DIVINE HEALING
MADE SIMPLE

D1310885

DIVINE HEALING
MADE SIMPLE

Simplifying the supernatural
to make healing and miracles
a part of your everyday life

Praying Medic

**INKITY
PRESS**™

© Copyright 2013 – Praying Medic

All rights reserved. This book is protected by the copyright laws of the United States of America. No portion of this book may be stored electronically, transmitted, copied, reproduced or reprinted for commercial gain or profit without prior written permission from Inkity Press™. Permission requests may be emailed to **admin@inkitypress.com** or sent to the Inkity Press mailing address below. Only the use of short quotations or occasional page copying for personal or group study is allowed without written permission.

Unless otherwise noted, all scripture quotations are taken from the New King James Version®. Copyright © 1982 by Thomas Nelson, Inc. Used by permission. All rights reserved.

Inkity Press™
137 East Elliot Road, #2292, Gilbert, AZ 85234

This book and other Inkity Press titles can be found at:
InkityPress.com and PrayingMedic.com

Available from Amazon.com, CreateSpace.com, and other retail outlets.

For more information visit our website at **www.inkitypress.com**
or email us at **admin@inkitypress.com** or **admin@prayingmedic.com**

ISBN-13: 978-0615937281 (Inkity Press)
ISBN-10: 0615937284

Printed in the U.S.A.

IT IS WITH BITTERSWEET JOY that I dedicate this book to my friend Scott Buzzell, who stepped into eternity this year after fighting the good fight against Lou Gehrig's disease. I look forward to playing that round of golf with you my friend, on the fairways of heaven.

FOREWORD

THERE ARE TWO TRENDS IN the Kingdom of God that are converging in this book. It's been evident for several years that God is doing something special with the topic of healing the sick. And it's been clear that God is taking His Church out of the buildings and into the streets. The result is that God has been performing a great many miracles of healing in shopping malls, on sidewalks, in the workplace, and yes, even in the back of ambulances. How fortuitous that He has given us this book as a tool to equip the saints for the work of this ministry.

What you hold in your hands is a powerful tool. These are not the musings of a professional theologian declaring, "Well, this is the way that it *should* work." These are not even the teachings of an experienced pastor declaring the path that the sheep should follow. This is not a superhero story.

Instead, this is practical, street-level advice from a regular guy, a Christian brother, who has found himself on the front lines of the 21st century's street-healing movement. He's a relatively new brother at that, and frankly, he's only been involved in healing the sick for a handful of years. In the last few years his success rate has risen to what he estimates is about 80 percent. Four times out of five, when he prays for the sick, God does something; the result is that the people he prays for are better than they were before prayer.

This is an accessible book: a "regular guy" facing "regular issues" has discovered some powerful insights in the road that God is taking us on, and he's sharing his story: "This is what has worked for me."

I am a wealthy man: I count the author, the Praying Medic, as a friend and co-laborer in the Kingdom. God introduced the two of us around the time that He first spoke to the Medic about healing the sick. I've watched him grow into this calling; I've cheered him on as he – with a generous handful of other pioneers around the western world – built and documented a trail for us to follow into this place where God is leading His people.

Praying Medic is qualified more than most people to lead us into this battle: He's doing the things he teaches, he's doing them *successfully*, and he's a real person, who shares that realness – both good and frustrating – of his journey with us. By the way, I measure his successes in two ways: first, people tend to find themselves healed when he prays for them, and second, people that hang out around him often find themselves healing the sick, successfully.

If I may be so bold, this book is not as much a teaching of how to "do the stuff" (as John Wimber used to say) of healing the sick, though there is plenty of excellent teaching in these pages. Rather, it is a testimony of what Jesus has done with and through one reluctant man. And as a testimony, Revelation 19:10 applies: "...For the testimony of Jesus is the spirit of prophecy." The things that the Medic is testifying about work as a prophecy in the life of the reader: God has done this before and He's ready to do it again, through you.

Are you ready for an adventure? Let's go!

~ Editor of *Northwest Prophetic.com*

ACKNOWLEDGMENTS

THERE ARE MANY PEOPLE I would like to thank for their contribution in making this book possible. This has truly been a group effort from start to finish. Literally hundreds of people have participated in the process by giving me feedback on my initial Facebook discussions about healing and by leaving comments and suggestions on the articles I wrote that became the basis for this book. I'm sorry that I can't thank all of you personally. If I don't mention your name, know that I greatly appreciate your help and your friendship.

Among the hundreds of friends I've met through Facebook that have given me feedback and encouragement, I'd like to mention a few folks who have stood beside me, day in and day out. These are the friends who have prayed for me and encouraged me every step of the way. They are people like Alan Champkins, Amie Larson, Amy Marten, Amy Rubeck, Ana Rosa Colon, Andi Trout Reese, Angela Langley, Anny Ruch, April Filitzke Gambino, April Smithee, Becky Haas, Belinda Marsh, Beverley Sparrow O'Flynn, Bill & Sandy Coultas, Bob Elligot, Bridgette Rodgers, Charlene Picard, Cheryl Chapman Rector, Christopher Huszar, Chrystal Spencer, Cindy DeGroot, Cindy Kay, Clint Mitchell, Corma Holmes, Dan

Hurd, Danielle Shelley, David Hunter, David Weekley, Deonna Crochet, Derrick Day, Diana Devlin, Diana Jamerson, Diane Eisenman Moyer, Donna Delaney, Duane Finnie, Elizabeth Keith, Eno Udoetuk, EstaAnn Ammerman, Etta Bowe, Garth Lange, Greg Hunter, Greg Kiser, Gregg Taylor, Gwen Polzin, Hannah Whalen, Hazel May Lebrun, Heather Goodman, Helle Stock, Imre Emanuel Mogheri, J. Linda Stevens, James and Andrea Fraser, James and Erin Marsee, Jane Bolen, Jeannie Fortuna, Jeff Wissler, Jennifer Middleton, Jim Brown, Jim Tedford, Joe Elligot, Jon Sellers, Josh Cosker, Jule Bedford, Karen McCune, Kari Clement, Kat Wells Anderson, Kaylani Steele, Kent Lindsay, Kevin Peacock, Kim O'Hara, Kim O'Keefe, Kim Pittman, Linda Blansett, Liz Adams, Lois Tatro, LouAnn Saltzman Engles, Lucy Parker, Luther Leser, Lyn Valentine, Mandy Madryga, Maria Victoria Bartlett, Marie Sonlight, Mark Stewart, Mark Williams, Meredith Martin, Michelle Liana, Nashville Kat, Natalie Myrick-Whittaker, Nikki Tucker, Nicole Joseph, Omotola Omogbolahan, Pat Hux, Paul and April Luna, Paul and Ginny Wilcox, Praise Egbon-relu, Ravi Kapoor, Rebecca Clayton, Regie Pfeiffer, Richard Murray, Rob Taylor, Robert Hankins, Roslyn Koelle, Sandra Weaver, Sharon Murrone Reece, Sharon Parkinson, Steve and Jennifer Dahlquist, Steve Henderson, Steve Mclean, Steve Moreland, Sue Beach, Sue Beckman, Sue Wilke, Susan Brown, Tarik Carey, Terri Guadalupe, Terry Ashcraft, Terry Mingus, Victoria Winterowd, Wanda Gladney, Wendy Huffman Hanely, Kathy and Schuler Murdock and Melissa Floyd.

I would also like to thank my peers – the men and women at the forefront of the new healing movement who have taught others about healing and encouraged me to write this book. Among them are: Anton Guerrero, Art Mongomery, Bob Hazlett, Bob Hynes, Brae Wyck-off, Brandon Lee, Cheryl Fritz, Chris Overstreet, Chris Villaflor, Colin Rice, Cornel Marais, Dan Mohler, Dennis and Diane Teague, Donald Mann, Eric Wilding, Eunice Bennett, Graeme Morris, Glen Hartline, Greg McCoy, Jason Chin, Jason Tax, Jeff Turner, Jason and Rachelle McCoy, Jesse Snow, Jessie Campbell, Joe Funaro, Joel Adifon, Joel Jackson, John Bridge, John Mellor, Josh Tongol, Joshua Greeson, Ken Nichols, Kriston Couchey, Lisa Adams, Marc and Lydia Buchheit, Melissa Glorioso, Nicole Joseph, Pete Cabrera Jr., Rafael Garcia, Roger Sapp, Roger Webb, Ryan Rhoades, Sherry Evans, Steve Bremner, Steve Harmon, Terry Chambers, Tom Fischer and Tom Ruotolo. Thank you all for your leadership in advancing the kingdom of God.

A handful of men have profoundly influenced me in my pursuit of understanding healing. I've spent hundreds of hours studying and gaining inspiration from their teachings. I recommend them to anyone wishing to walk in the power of God. They are Cal Pierce, Randy Clark, Todd White and Bill Johnson.

I would like to thank the following people who have helped me in their own unique ways:

Lydia Conrad – who graciously agreed to be my editor. Editing can be a thankless job, but her work makes my writing more readable. I'm fortunate to have someone who was willing to devote hours of time to reviewing the manuscript and suggesting changes to the content and style. It was a challenge being asked to re-write large sections of some of the chapters, but because she was not satisfied with anything less than my best effort, the end result is a much more readable book. I greatly appreciate her skills, time and effort.

Matt Evans – for taking me under his wing when I first became interested in healing. He was my first mentor in healing and his encouragement was needed when I saw no success early on. His insights have helped me to better understand the ways of God.

Tyler Johnson – for taking the time to share his experiences with publishing, which helped me move forward with publishing this book.

Paula Otano and Melody Paasch – for helping me, my wife, and many others, better understand dream interpretation and the prophetic.

Christina Klover – for the many encouraging prophetic words to me and my friends when we so badly needed them.

The Graceful Banker – who followed my website for about a year, reading my stories about healing. He invited me come to Australia with my wife to teach his friends about the miraculous. From the moment we met at the airport, a new friendship blossomed. Though he lives on the other side of the planet, we keep in touch often and he's become one of my best friends. I owe him a debt of gratitude for becoming my "person of peace."

Denise Hayes – for her design talent on the cover art and book interior. I'm extremely happy with the results of her work.

Michael King – for his friendship, love and encouragement. Michael has always provided a safe backdrop for me to think outside the box regarding spiritual matters. Whenever I had a dream where the Holy Spirit revealed something about healing that I had never thought of, Michael was there to help interpret the dream and bring clarity to the issue and for that I am grateful.

Craig Adams – for being a brother and a spiritual father to me. I consider Craig to be a mentor, but he's never treated me as anything less than an equal. He has always encouraged me to let the Holy Spirit teach me the deeper things of the kingdom. His maturity and wisdom have been a great help in writing this book.

Todd Adams – a warrior with a drum and a spiritual brother. I've leaned on him many times over the years. His warm, down to earth way of seeing Jesus has helped me to see Him the way He really is.

Editor of Northwest Prophetic – for being a friend and the instrument God used to open my eyes to the realities of His kingdom. Before meeting him, I had no concept of what the kingdom was. All I knew about was "the church." He mentored me for years and encouraged me to pursue whatever God was doing in my life, regardless of how strange it seemed. Were it not for his friendship and patient instruction, this book would not be in your hands.

Finally, I would like to thank my wife, who probably has as much time invested in this book as I do. She's been my best friend, my counselor, and biggest encourager. She spent countless hours helping with the first round of editing and proofreading. She has helped me with the many prayer requests I've received through Facebook and my website and she's helped decode the dreams I've had about healing. She's an amazing woman and without her love and support, I probably would have given up on the book long ago. Thanks honey – you're the best.

~ Praying Medic

TABLE OF CONTENTS

NOTE

Although I work as a trained paramedic, I am not a physician. I cannot diagnose diseases or recommend the best course of medical treatment for them. The advice given in this book is not intended to replace the advice of a medical doctor or other licensed health care professional. I do not assume liability for any harm that results from a decision to forego medical treatment. I cannot guarantee that the suggestions given in this book will result in the same outcomes I, or others, have experienced. I am not responsible for the outcomes that result from following the advice given in this book. There is no guarantee that the teaching in this book will lead to healing. While I believe wholeheartedly in divine healing, I also believe in and encourage you to seek standard diagnostic testing and medical treatment if it is indicated.

INTRODUCTION

ON THE STREETS OF LOS Angeles, Steve Harmon spends his days meeting with friends, healing their illnesses, and teaching them how to release the power of God.

In Great Bend, Kansas, Pete Cabrera Jr. runs a soup kitchen. The sick and crippled come in. They leave healthy and sound. Hundreds have been healed through this ordinary man who has a passion for seeing the sick made well.

In Perth, Australia, Jessie Campbell releases the power of God on the town's people each day while walking to the market. People are set free of demonic oppression. The sick are miraculously healed and God's love is openly displayed for all to see.

In Atlantic City, New Jersey, my friend Tom Fischer strolls the board-walk healing the sick, casting out demons and bringing strangers into a relationship with God. When the healed person stands in stunned amazement, trying to comprehend what just happened, Tom asks, "Ain't that crazy?"

In Denmark, Helle Stock, a new believer walks the streets with a friend, healing dislocated shoulders and injured backs. She's been a Christian for 22 days. She's never read the Bible or taken a ministry class.

In San Jose, California, Jose Coelho and his friends visit the waiting room of a hospital emergency department. They announce that Jesus will heal anyone who wants to be healed. Those who speak up are healed and leave the hospital.

In Tacoma, Washington, a patient is diagnosed with life threatening internal bleeding in the emergency department. Six units of blood are transfused and an ambulance is called to transport him to another hospital for surgery. The paramedic prays with him during the transport. Upon arriving at the other hospital, no sign of bleeding can be found and the man is sent home.

There is a movement sweeping the globe today. It's a wave of thousands of average people like you and I, who are releasing the healing power of God in everyday situations. These people are electricians, plumbers, waitresses, truck drivers, insurance salesmen, counselors, paramedics, college students and stay at home moms. Some are ex-drug addicts and some have criminal records. Few of them have been ordained into ministry or attended a seminary. In the eyes of most people, they are completely unqualified to do what they're doing. Yet they're touching strangers with the power of God everywhere they go.

What amazes me about this movement isn't just the fact that ordinary people are being used by God to do miracles, it's the consistency of healing being reported. Over the last five years I have read and watched on video over 1,000 testimonies from the healed and the healers. Among the most active healers, the reported success rates are over 80 percent. These aren't inflated estimates or wishful thinking. Many of the healings have been recorded on video and posted for public scrutiny.

Why do we need another book on healing?

When you read the pages of scripture, you'll find dozens of accounts of people who were healed by Jesus, the disciples or the Old Testament prophets. Healing stories are numerous, but what you won't find is instruction on *how* these healings were done.

There are no explanations as to why Jesus put mud in the eye of one blind man, touched the eyes of another, and told a third that his faith had restored his sight. Jesus never explained why He healed the way He did. The New Testament writers were mostly silent on the hows and whys of healing. Most people who have had success in healing developed their own methods and theories as why one way works better than another.

Most people who have prayed for healing have wondered why some people were healed, while others were not. Some have had their symptoms reappear, with no explanation as to why. This book will answer these questions and many others.

This book began as a series of articles, which I posted online. I received a lot of positive feedback on the articles. One comment I heard often was that my explanations took the complex subject of healing and explained it in a way that was simple to understand. When my wife and I were trying to come up with a title for the book, we chose the words "divine healing made simple" because we believe that simplicity is the thing that makes this book different from other books on healing. Rather than confuse you with religious jargon, my goal is to take the mystery out of healing and make things as simple as possible.

My reason for writing this book is to train average people to heal the sick outside the walls of the church. Until recently, healing has been confined mostly to times of prayer during church services, healing conferences and evangelistic crusades. Most of the people involved are in full time ministry. Average people like you and I haven't participated much. Healing in the workplace and in health care has been almost non-existent. The aim of this book is to teach you to use healing in virtually any setting.

The first half of the book provides background information for those who are new to healing. The later chapters are full of practical tips on how to operate in healing no matter where you are. We'll examine the most successful approaches to healing and point out common mistakes people make. We'll look at strategies for using healing where you work and in the medical field. If you put the things you learn into practice, this book will radically change your life and the lives of those around you.

My Story

If you consider the type of people who write books on healing, I'll admit – I'm probably the least qualified candidate. I was an atheist for most of my life. At the age of 38, I became a Christian. As a new believer I listened to Bible teachers, but I rejected healing and the supernatural. I particularly mistrusted faith healers, who I saw as phonies or con-men. I'm not a theologian. I don't have a college degree. I've never been ordained into ministry or even taken a ministry class. I've never pastored a church. Why would anyone read a book written by such an unqualified person?

Since 1982, I've worked in the field of emergency medicine; the majority of that time as a paramedic. After decades of seeing trauma, death and suffering on a daily basis, my heart cried out to God to do something about it. He heard my cry and answered in an unexpected way.

I've never had dreams as an adult. On August 8th in 2008, God appeared to me in the first dream I had in 25 years. Although I did not see God in the dream, I heard Him speak. He said, "I want you to pray with your patients. I'll show you what is wrong with them. And when you pray, I will heal them."

He then showed me a series of visions where I saw myself praying with patients, co-workers and hospital staff. At the time, I did not believe God still healed people. Since that night, I've had more than 200 dreams about the subject of healing. In each one, God revealed something about how healing works. Much of what I'll share in this book comes directly from those dreams.

After I began having dreams about healing, I reluctantly started praying with my patients. Wavering between belief and skepticism I prayed for about 500 people during the next six months but I didn't see anyone healed. I found it hard to continue praying when no one was being healed. I needed something to motivate me. I thought that if I wrote my stories on a blog, I'd be forced to pray with people so I would have something to write about. It was a case of backward thinking, but it worked. I kept praying and eventually the healing testimonies came in. Since 2008, I've authored a website, where I share stories about the people I've prayed with and seen healed.

The website motivated me to pray, but it also gave me the opportunity to post stories from others who operate in healing. It grew in popularity and through social networking sites like Facebook and Twitter, it connected me to thousands of people involved in healing around the world. During this time, my private identity has remained anonymous. Nearly all these friends know me only as "Praying Medic."

My role in all of this has been to verify and publish healing testimonies, teach beginners how to operate in healing and facilitate discussions on healing. On my Facebook page, I've asked just about every question imaginable about healing, eliciting responses from skeptics and experienced healers alike. The comments run into the hundreds, with discussions lasting anywhere from a few days to a few weeks.

This book can't provide the answer to every question about healing. I still have many unanswered questions myself. During the writing of this book, I revised the manuscript frequently as more pieces of the healing puzzle dropped into place. I know that after the book goes to print, more answers will come to light. Healing, like medicine, is a body of knowledge that is continually expanding as we make new discoveries. This book is a snapshot in time, an incomplete glimpse of what we've learned so far. My hope is to share what we know today and encourage you to begin your own journey of discovery.

CHAPTER ONE

Misconceptions and Myths about Healing

BEING A FORMER ATHEIST AND a person who flatly rejected healing a few years ago, I appreciate honest skepticism. While childlike faith is admirable, few of us are able to hold onto the simplicity of believing in miracles as we grow older. Most of us are exposed to fraud somewhere along the way and it hardens us little by little.

Miracles, especially those that come by faith, are not rational. That is to say that the miraculous does not appeal to the rational mind. When we see a sudden change in something, our mind wants to know what caused it. For example, if you observed a kettle of water boiling, you would not assume it was caused by a miracle. You would investigate other causes first. When a miracle is suggested as the cause of something, every other explanation should be ruled out first. A miracle is never the most likely cause of anything. It should be the last thing considered after other explanations have been eliminated.

The miracles of Jesus are the subject of this book. The carpenter from Nazareth understood skepticism and He expected it. His miracles were a challenge to the skeptics of His day. Skepticism is normal for those who are unfamiliar with the miraculous. But when we're exposed to things that defy natural explanation, we must begin to consider supernatural explanations. When the miracles of Jesus were observed, the crowd was forced to admit, based on the evidence they saw with their own eyes, "Surely this man was sent from God, for no one could do such things unless God was with Him." When we witness one miracle after another and harden our heart against the evidence, the choice to remain a skeptic destroys our ability to reason.

If you're a skeptic, you need not believe in miracles without seeing them firsthand. I urge you to find people who claim to be working miracles and see them for yourself. These days they aren't hard to find. Many of them have YouTube channels and do their healing in public. Interview those who are healed and the ones doing the healing and ask them the hard questions to satisfy your need to know the truth.

I've spent the last few years doing exactly that. I've listened to the testimonies and objections from believers and skeptics. We've discussed nearly every aspect of healing, including why some people are more successful at healing, why some people aren't healed, why people "lose" their healing, whether there is clinical evidence to support the claims of healing and different views about God's will for healing. Unless you settle your mind on these matters, you have virtually no chance of seeing people healed. Healing comes by faith. Faith is destroyed by doubt. If you doubt whether God wants people to be healed, you won't see them healed. I won't ask you to believe everything in this book merely because I wrote it. I only ask that you weigh the evidence and settle the issue in your mind. If the arguments for healing lack merit, then dismiss them. If they hold up under scrutiny, then believe them and move on to the next step, which is growing in faith and seeing people healed.

If you spend time with those who heal the sick, you're going to hear a number of objections to and myths about healing. The remainder of this chapter will address some of the most common ones you're likely to encounter.

"Healing ceased in the first century with the passing of the apostles or after Scripture was established."

Divine healing has been the rightful domain of the Church for two thousand years. But in the centuries following the death of Jesus, healing became a rare thing. Over time, some church leaders adopted the view that healing ended in the first century or soon afterward, when the New Testament Scriptures were completed. Supporters of this view argue that it was at this point that healing was no longer needed to verify the preaching of the gospel and the practice of healing ceased. This view became known as *cessationism*. It became a dominant view and is still popular today.

"What about Paul's 'thorn in the flesh'?"

The argument against healing can't be made from the plain teaching of Scripture itself. You can scour the New Testament from Matthew to Revelation and not find a single verse plainly teaching that healing would ever cease. The best a cessationist can do is to argue against healing by inference; that is by inferring into a passage a meaning that is not obvious to the reader. The most commonly heard objection to healing is Paul's thorn in the flesh. Let's look at Paul's commentary on this issue:

> *And lest I should be exalted above measure by the abundance of the revelations, a thorn in the flesh was given to me, a messenger of Satan to buffet me, lest I be exalted above measure.*
> 2 COR. 12:7

Cessationists argue that Paul's "thorn in the flesh" was a form of sickness that he asked God to remove and God refused to do it. From this they argue that God may want us to be sick for various reasons. There are several problems with this line of reasoning. The first is that sickness is not discussed plainly in this passage. If one believes that Paul was discussing sickness, it must be inferred into the text, because the plain rendering does not give that meaning. The second problem that cessationists must overcome is that the obvious subject of the chapter is persecution – not sickness. In this passage, Paul illustrates his teaching on persecution with a personal example, focusing for a moment on the persecution he suffered for the revelation he received from God. He stated that in order to keep him from being exalted too highly, God allowed Satan to send a messenger to harass him. Notice; there is no mention of sickness.

When you examine the Greek text, there is no indication that the messenger Paul referred to was a form of sickness. The Greek word for "messenger" in this passage is *aggelos*, which is usually translated "angel." The obvious meaning would be that Satan sent a fallen angel (or perhaps a demon) to harass Paul, which God permitted to keep him humble. There is no reason to believe this passage supports the idea that God would not heal him of sickness.

The other argument used against healing is the observation that sickness was present among early church leaders such as Paul, Timothy and Epaphroditus. Cessationists point to the presence of sickness as evidence that healing began to decline and eventually ceased, causing the Church to live with sickness as the "apostolic age" came to a close.

Let's look at the sickness of Epaphroditus, which Paul mentions in his letter to the Philippians:

> *Yet I considered it necessary to send to you Epaphroditus, my brother, fellow worker, and fellow soldier, but your messenger and the one who ministered to my need; since he was longing for you all, and was distressed because you had heard that he was sick. For indeed he was sick almost unto death; but God had mercy on him, and not only on him but on me also, lest I should have sorrow upon sorrow. Therefore I sent him the more eagerly, that when you see him again you may rejoice, and I may be less sorrowful.*
> PHIL. 2:25-28

It is true that Epaphroditus suffered sickness, even to the point of near death. But if we want to know whether healing had ceased, we must determine if he was healed or not. After describing his sickness in verse 27, Paul says, "but God had mercy on him."

What did Paul mean? It's impossible to say with certainty, but the tone suggests an unexpected outcome. Paul writes, "Epaphroditus was sick... but God had mercy on him." The natural conclusion one would come to was that after a serious battle with illness, Epaphroditus was healed. Paul then writes that he sent Epaphroditus so that the believers in Philippi might rejoice upon seeing him. Would Paul send a friend who was nearly dead thinking that it would cause them to rejoice?

A more logical explanation would be that after Epaphroditus was healed, Paul was able to send him, knowing that when they saw him healed they would rejoice. Rather than suggesting that healing had ceased, this passage confirms that healing was still in operation. Now let's look at Timothy's illness and Paul's prescription for it:

> *No longer drink only water, but use a little wine for your stomach's sake and your frequent infirmities.*
> 1 TIM. 5:23

In this brief passage, Paul notes that Timothy's infirmities were a result of drinking only water. We don't know the reason why the water he drank made him sick. It's possible that it was contaminated, giving him some type of bacterial infection. Paul's antidote was to have him drink a little wine. The infirmities were not severe enough that they required healing. Paul confidently explains that the illness would resolve if he refrained from drinking only water. This passage in no way indicates that God would not heal Timothy. It's merely the case of an older and wiser man instructing a younger one to take some practical steps to avoid becoming sick.

The New Testament does not show a decrease in the effectiveness of healing as critics suppose. The disciples were still healing all who were sick and demon-possessed as recorded in the book of Acts:

> *And believers were increasingly added to the Lord, multitudes of both men and women, so that they brought the sick out into the streets and laid them on beds and couches, that at least the shadow of Peter passing by might fall on some of them. Also a multitude gathered from the surrounding cities to Jerusalem, bringing sick people and those who were tormented by unclean spirits, and they were all healed.*
> ACTS 5:14-16

"There is sickness in the Church."

It has been suggested that because members of the church were sick, God must not have been willing to heal them. In response, I'd like to make this observation: I know hundreds of people who successfully operate in healing today and nearly all of them suffer from sickness once in a while. The presence of sickness among a group of people does not prove that healing isn't also happening among them. On the contrary, in order for healing to occur, sickness must be present.

The argument against healing is not supported by the works of the early church. Instead, we find that Jesus and His disciples demonstrated and taught that operating in the healing power of God was the expected, normal lifestyle for every believer and they gave no indication that healing would ever cease.

We should also consider the fact that many people are receiving healing today. Every year tens of thousands of people receive miraculous healing that is documented as such by physicians. If these things were supposed to have ceased, we might ask why so many people are still experiencing them?

Finally, there is the idea that healing was intended only as a means to support the spread of the gospel and that healing ceased because it was no longer needed. Jesus commissioned His disciples to heal as they preached but He never suggested that healing would cease to be used this way. Furthermore, healing isn't just a means to verify a message. It's a tangible demonstration of God's power, love, mercy and compassion, a means of warfare against the kingdom of darkness, a means of making people spiritually, physically and emotionally whole and a way to bring people into a personal relationship with God.

"I don't have the gift of healing."

This is a commonly held view and it's understandable, given what most people know about healing. It comes from the observation that healing is done by only a few people and that the ones doing it must be special in some way. Although healing miracles haven't been abundant, they have been reported throughout the entire church age. Because of their scarcity, the practice of healing fell into obscurity and people wondered why. The honest answer would be to admit that the Church had strayed from the commission Jesus had given it. But admitting error is painful. Some leaders chose instead to invent explanations justifying the absence of healing. And this is what is taught in many congregations today. The truth is that the demise of healing came as a result of disobedience to the instructions of Jesus and nothing more.

On the rare occasion when someone did manage to operate in healing, the people who saw it came to one of two conclusions. Some thought the healers were frauds because healing wasn't being done by respected religious leaders. They vilified the "fraudulent healers" and developed doctrines against healing.

Those who accepted healing believed that God had imparted a special gift to that person. The special person nearly always became the object of attention and would earn legendary status; their names being inscribed forever in the minds of our culture; men and women like John G. Lake, Smith Wigglesworth, Amiee Semple McPherson and Benny Hinn.

The truth is – both of these conclusions are wrong. These men and women deserve neither the criticism nor the acclaim they've received. They weren't given a special gift. They were simply walking in the power that's been available to every believer all along. The only real difference between the man on the platform and you is that he believes God wants to heal the sick and he acts on that belief, and you probably don't. But you could, with a little faith and obedience.

If you are interested in healing, there is only one prerequisite. The power and authority to heal the sick is given to the disciples of Jesus. If you aren't His disciple yet, you should become one. Ask Him to come into your life and the Spirit of God will come and dwell in you.

If you are a believer, the power and authority are already yours. Jesus commissioned His disciples to heal the sick, raise the dead, cast out demons and proclaim the kingdom. This power and authority is given to every disciple of Jesus (see Mt. 10:7-8 and Lk. 10: 1-9).

There is however, a true gift of healing as described in 1 Corinthians chapter 12. We'll discuss this in detail in another chapter, but briefly, the gift of healing is not the same as the authority given to believers to heal the sick. The gifts of the Holy Spirit are primarily for building up and strengthening other believers. Healing and miracles are included in those gifts. Paul taught that not all believers would operate in every spiritual gift, so in a sense the gift of healing may not be operational in every believer. In contrast to the gift of healing, the believer's authority to heal is tied to the proclamation of the gospel. Jesus expected all of His disciples to proclaim the gospel and healing the sick goes along with that. If you are one of His disciples, you have the same authority to heal as any other believer.

"Men can't heal the sick, only God can heal them."

When I say that one of my friends healed a sick person, I sometimes hear the objection, "We can't heal the sick, only God can do that." This is another understandable objection, but it's best to look at what the Bible says.

If you asked a group of Christians who it was that multiplied the loaves of bread and fishes to feed the multitude, the majority would say it was Jesus. And the majority would be wrong. If you look closely at the passage that describes this event, you'll notice a few details that are often overlooked. When the multitude grew hungry and the disciples asked if they should send the crowd away, Jesus gave them a challenge, saying, "You give them something to eat." A bit perplexed, they found a boy who had a few fish and some bread. They gave the bread and fish to Jesus, who blessed it, broke it and handed it back to them. When He gave it back to them, it had not yet multiplied. The disciples began to hand out the food and as they distributed it, it began to multiply in their own hands. It was in the hands of the disciples that the miracle took place, not in the hands of Jesus (see Jn. 6:5-13).

A small error it may be, but the revelation we have from the correct perspective shows that the disciples were capable of working greater miracles than they knew. Jesus challenged them to do the miraculous works of God in the same manner He did. In Luke chapter 10, He told them to heal the sick, cast out demons, raise the dead and proclaim the kingdom. So allow me to ask a few questions:

If the kingdom of God was proclaimed by the disciples, who was responsible for doing it? The answer is, "the disciples." No one would say that God proclaimed the message of the gospel, because believers proclaim the gospel.

If demons were cast out by the disciples, who was responsible for doing it? For the same reason we would say the disciples proclaimed the gospel, we would say they cast out demons. Although the power of God is used to do it, God does not cast out demons. It is done by disciples.

If the sick were healed by the disciples, who was responsible? Once again, it would be the disciples.

And if the dead were raised by the disciples, who would be responsible for doing it? The disciples.

We use the power of God to do all these things; even proclaiming the gospel, for "The gospel is the power of God unto salvation" (see Rom 1:16). God is the one who receives the glory for the works that we do. But the fact remains that Jesus told His disciples to heal the sick. He did not tell them to ask the Father to heal the sick. He told them to do it. When a disciple obeys and healing happens, it is not wrong to say the disciple did the healing.

When I use the term "healer" in this book, I'm not implying that "healer" is a special title or privilege given only to a few people. It is the right and responsibility of every believer. The term "healer" as I use it, merely refers to someone who happens to be active in healing, as opposed to someone who could be, but is not.

"God is developing my character."

There exists a widely-held belief that God uses sickness to teach us lessons and develop character. Although I once held this view, let me explain why I no longer do. Many people point to the life of Job as an example of how God uses sickness and affliction to build character. The first assertion made is that God makes people sick, so let's examine this idea.

In the second chapter of the book of Job, Satan came to ask God for permission to afflict Job with sickness (see Job 2:3-6). God granted Satan's request and put limitations on it. He would be allowed to afflict Job with sickness, take away his wealth and even kill Job's family, but he was not allowed to kill Job. After receiving permission, Satan put his plan into action:

> *So Satan went out from the presence of the LORD, and struck Job with painful boils from the sole of his foot to the crown of his head.*
> JOB 2:7

From this passage we can see that sickness, disease and even death are planned and carried out by Satan and not God. While God may give Satan and his minions permission to do things like tempting us to sin or giving us sickness, His permission should not be viewed as approval of them and we should not accuse God of making us sick or causing us to die. The agent of sickness and death is Satan.

Satan wanted to make Job sick, take his wealth and destroy his family because he believed Job would curse God if he did. But the Lord knew the whole time Job wouldn't curse Him and even told Satan so. He boasted to Satan that Job was a man of great character before Satan attacked him. Job's sickness and afflictions didn't build character; they revealed the character he already had.

I'm not suggesting that the Bible teaches that all sickness and pain have spiritual causes or that they all come from Satan. Some of the things we suffer from are nothing more than the effects of physics and poor choices. Many obese people who suffer from diabetes have their blood sugar return to normal after losing weight. Peptic ulcers often clear up after the individual quits their stressful job that caused it. Industrial diseases can be cured in some cases by leaving the toxic environment. God does not afflict us with sickness, Satan does. But not all sickness is from Satan; some of it is self-inflicted.

Now let's look at some of the most common reasons I've heard people give for not being healed.

"I'm not good enough to be healed."

In this section, I'll refer to the passage below where Jesus healed a number of people:

> *And he came down with them and stood on a level place, with a great crowd of His disciples and a great multitude of people from all Judea and Jerusalem and the seacoast of Tyre and Sidon, who came to hear him and to be healed of their diseases. And those who were troubled with unclean spirits were cured. And all the crowd sought to touch him, for power came out from him and healed them all.*
>
> LK. 6:17-19

If you believe that you haven't been healed because you aren't good enough in God's eyes, allow me to ask, how many righteous people do you suppose Jesus healed in this large crowd? Consider that demonized people are often involved in drug use and idol worship, yet Jesus healed and delivered all of them. This was probably a group of average people such as you'd find on the streets of any city in the world. None of them were righteous enough to deserve healing, because healing isn't based on how good we are. Healing is an act of God's grace, just like salvation.

There are three biblical principles I'd like to mention briefly; they are justice, mercy and grace. Justice is receiving what we deserve. Most of us like justice as long as it's not being measured out to us. Mercy is when God withholds the justice we deserve for our wrongdoing. Grace is when God gives us something we don't deserve. Salvation and healing are acts of mercy and grace. Concerning God's grace, the apostle Paul wrote:

> *For it is by grace you have been saved, through faith, not of works, that no one should boast.*
>
> EPH. 2:8

The word "saved" in this verse is the Greek word *sozo*, which means to save, preserve, protect, heal or make whole. Healing is one of the ways in which the grace of God is revealed to us. I sometimes receive prayer requests where a relative cites a long list of good deeds done by the person they want me to pray for. They do this because they believe that people who lead a life of sacrifice or service to others are somehow more deserving of healing than those who do not. Thankfully, neither our good deeds nor our bad ones matter when grace is at work. God's grace can never be earned. It is a free gift. All we can do is receive it. As someone who needs healing, you're a candidate to be healed, regardless of your beliefs or lifestyle. No one is outside the reach of God's grace for healing except those who don't want to be healed.

"We will all be healed in heaven."

This belief comes from the idea that our physical bodies are bound to suffer sickness and damage in this life and that once we are in heaven, our bodies will be healed. There is an assumption made here, that we will have physical bodies in heaven. We must ask then, "Do we have physical bodies in heaven that can receive healing?"

The answer is no. The apostle Paul teaches in a number of places that there are two kinds of bodies. We have a physical body for this life and a spiritual one for eternity:

> *The body is sown in corruption, it is raised in incorruption. It is sown in dishonor, it is raised in glory. It is sown in weakness, it is raised in power. It is sown a natural body, it is raised a spiritual body. There is a natural body, and there is a spiritual body... For this corruptible must put on incorruption, and this mortal must put on immortality.*
> 1 COR. 15:42-44 AND 53

Our physical bodies do not go with us in eternity. In heaven, we will receive a spiritual body that is created for our eternal existence – one that does not become sick or injured; therefore our physical bodies cannot be healed after we die. If our bodies are to receive the healing God has provided for us, it can only be received while we are alive.

"An atmosphere of unbelief prevents healing."

A popular teaching in the Charismatic church is that when a strong attitude of unbelief is present among a group of people, it creates an environment of unbelief. It is taught that when this type of environment is present, the healing work of God is blocked by the "atmosphere of unbelief." Adherents support this teaching by quoting the following passage where Matthew noted that Jesus did not perform many miracles in His hometown:

Now He did not do many mighty works there because of their unbelief.
MT. 13:58

If we took this passage at face value, we might agree that an attitude of unbelief prevents miracles from happening. But let's look at another passage that describes the scene in more detail. This parallel passage notes that Jesus did heal a few people in His hometown:

Now He could do no mighty work there, except that He laid His hands on a few sick people and healed them.
MK. 6:5

If the work of God is restricted by a corporate attitude of unbelief then how did Jesus heal these people?

In the cities of Judea, Jesus was regarded as a man of God who taught with authority and had the power to do miracles. Many sought Him for healing because they understood who He was. But in His hometown of Nazareth, He was regarded as just another one of Joseph's sons. They knew Him from childhood and didn't regard Him as a miracle worker. Many of the townspeople were offended by Him and doubted His claims; they were full of unbelief. The people of His hometown could have experienced the same miracles Jesus did elsewhere. But their unbelief kept them from bringing the sick to Him for healing, thus it was said, "He did not do many mighty works because of their unbelief." It wasn't because His power was restricted; it was because they didn't ask Him to do the miracles out of their own unbelief (see Jn. 6:42 and Lk. 4:21-30).

"I don't have enough faith to be healed."

A few people mentioned in the Bible obtained healing by their own faith. The woman healed of a bleeding disorder, which she had for twelve years, is one example (see Mt. 9:22), but the majority of those healed by Jesus and the disciples had little or no faith. The only time Jesus ever told anyone they didn't have enough faith was when He reprimanded His disciples for their faithlessness when they couldn't cast a demon out of a boy who had epilepsy (see Mt. 17:17).

As the one who needs healing, it doesn't hurt to have faith, but it isn't necessary. What you need is the desire to be healed. Healing comes by faith and in the majority of cases, it's the faith of the one praying that determines the outcome. Sometimes when healing doesn't appear to manifest, the would-be healer will accuse the one who is sick of not having enough faith. Don't fall for this blame shifting tactic.

"I don't believe in Jesus."

Healing doesn't require the sick person to believe in Jesus or even in God, because healing is intended to make believers out of those who witness or receive it. Jesus told people to believe in Him because of the miracles He did. He didn't require them to believe before being healed:

> *"Believe Me that I am in the Father and the Father in Me, or else believe Me for the sake of the works themselves."*
> JN. 14:11

God often heals those we least expect because His grace and mercy are intended for everyone. Pete Cabrera visited the UK in April of 2011 to do some street healing. While in London, he met a man in a pub who was an atheist. Pete learned that the man suffered from chronic back pain. (One of the most common causes of low back pain is a misalignment of the hips due to one leg being longer than the other.) Pete asked the man to sit in a chair and extend his legs. He found that one leg was shorter, so Pete commanded it to grow. The legs became equal in length, which healed the back pain. The man became a follower of Jesus before he left the pub.

Sometimes healing miracles can even draw an observer into belief in God as this story of mine demonstrates:

In September of 2011, I transported a woman in my ambulance who complained of numbness in her right leg from her groin to her toes. Her doctor ordered an ultrasound, suspecting a vascular injury. She'd had a heart attack and stent placement a few weeks earlier.

(To insert a stent, they place a large needle and sheath into a blood vessel in the groin and advance it to the heart. Our suspicion was that the insertion site for the catheter in her groin may have developed an aneurysm, compressing the femoral nerve, causing numbness to her leg.)

To complicate the picture, she had end-stage kidney failure and was on dialysis. The dialysis fistula in her left arm deteriorated to the point where it was no longer useful. So her surgeon tied it off and following the surgery, she developed pain and some loss of function in her left hand. She also had complete blindness in her left eye and partial blindness in her right eye from detached retinas.

She lived at a nearby facility across the parking lot from the hospital. I had a few hundred feet of blacktop in which to work a miracle. As we wheeled her toward the elevator, I asked if she'd let me pray for her. She agreed, so I started with her left hand. She reported the pain as six out of ten. As we got on the elevator, I commanded the pain to leave in the name of Jesus. After the door closed, I asked how she felt.

"I don't feel anything, now."

"Do you feel any pain in your arm or hand?"

Smiling, and flexing her wrist and fingers in amazement, she said, "No pain at all. It feels normal."

Wheeled her toward the ambulance, we loaded the gurney. I needed to get her vital signs and call the receiving hospital. I asked my partner to get in back for a few minutes. I did a neurological assessment of her right leg. She felt nothing when I ran my finger along the sole of her foot. I did it several times to make sure. I pinched her skin above the ankle.

"I can feel you touching me, but I can't tell if it's dull or sharp."

Just below her knee, she could tell that I was pinching her skin. As I tested her ability to sense pain in her leg, I could tell that her neurological deficit was slight at the knee, progressively getting worse toward the foot, which had no sensation at all.

I placed my hand on her leg and invited the Holy Spirit to touch her, then commanded the nerves and blood vessels to be healed in the name of Jesus. I asked if she felt anything.

With a smile she replied, "My whole leg is tingling."

I rubbed the bottom of her foot again and asked if she felt anything.

"Yes, I can feel you touching the bottom of my foot." I pinched the skin above her ankle. "I can feel you pinching me." All the numbness in her leg was now gone.

My EMT partner, who had never worked with me before and had never seen a miracle, looked on in quiet amazement. The silence was broken when she finally said, "I think you may have just made a believer out of me."

CHAPTER TWO

The Biblical Basis for Healing

HEALING IS THE SUBJECT OF much debate, both inside and outside the church. There are many skeptics who would challenge the validity of divine healing. Some doubt healing itself, insisting that there is no clinical evidence demonstrating that healing is a real phenomenon. Others challenge the idea of healing as a biblical principle that is valid for today. In this chapter, we'll survey the most relevant passages of Scripture showing that healing is not only relevant today, but that it's a biblical imperative.

The Old Testament is rich with passages that teach the people of God about His character and nature. Each of God's names, which are found in the Old Testament, describe something about Him that was unknown at the time. In Exodus 15:26, God revealed that one of His names is, "Jehovah Rapha"... *"I AM the LORD, who heals you."* The literal translation of this name is: *"I AM your healing."* Healing is one of God's unchanging attributes, and although God's plans may change, He himself never changes (see Mal. 3:6). If God's nature was to heal then, it is still His nature to heal today.

When God's people rebelled against Him, serpents entered their camp. God told Moses to make a serpent of brass and put it on a pole in the middle of the camp and anyone who looked at it would be healed. God made a way for people to escape death and be healed. All they had to do was turn their eyes upon the brass serpent. Many did, but some did not. Healing has always been like this. It is available to all who desire to be healed, but it is never forced upon anyone (see Num. 21:8-9).

Before He was crucified, Jesus compared the death He would suffer to the time when Moses lifted up the brass serpent in the wilderness:

> *And as Moses lifted up the serpent in the wilderness, even so must the Son of Man be lifted up, that whoever believes in Him should not perish but have eternal life. For God so loved the world that He gave His only begotten Son, that whoever believes in Him should not perish but have everlasting life. For God did not send His Son into the world to condemn the world, but that the world through Him might be saved.*
> JN. 3:14-17

Jesus came to give His life as a ransom for many. His death demonstrated God's unconditional love for us and His desire to forgive sin. He came to reconcile those who were alienated and redeem that which was lost. He came to teach those who lived in darkness and to reveal the Father's heart to His creation. Nowhere is God's mercy and compassion more clearly demonstrated than in the healing miracles performed by the Rabbi who called himself the "Son of Man."

When Jesus suffered beating and death on the cross, not only did He obtain salvation for us, but He obtained our healing. In Isaiah 53, the prophet declared the things the Messiah would suffer and how His suffering would benefit us:

> *Surely he has borne our griefs and carried our sorrows; yet we esteemed him stricken, smitten by God, and afflicted. But he was*

wounded for our transgressions; he was crushed for our iniquities; upon him was the chastisement that brought us peace, and with his stripes we are healed. All we like sheep have gone astray; we have turned – every one – to his own way; and the LORD has laid on him the iniquity of us all.

ISA 53:4-6, NIV

In this passage Isaiah sees four things that are taken from us:

• Our griefs
• Our sorrows
• Our transgressions
• Our iniquities

He sees two things that are given to us:

• Peace
• Healing

With His suffering and death, Jesus purchased not only our freedom from sin, but our freedom from sickness. Notice the actions in this verse; the prophet saw our transgressions and iniquities being taken from us at the same time peace and healing were given to us. If the suffering and death of Jesus purchased our forgiveness of sin, they also purchased our healing. Forgiveness and healing are eternally tied together at the cross.

Forgiveness and healing are tied together in other places in Scripture. Jesus connected them in the following account from the gospel of Mark:

"Which is easier, to say to the paralytic, 'Your sins are forgiven you,' or to say, 'Arise, take up your bed and walk'? But that you may know that the Son of Man has power on earth to forgive sins" He said to the paralytic, *"I say to you, arise, take up your bed, and go to your house."*

MK. 2:9-11

While it's true that Jesus used this encounter as a visible demonstration of His authority to forgive sin, it also illustrates the relationship between forgiveness of sin and healing. Jesus has the same authority over both sin and sickness and the grace of God deals with them in the same way. With the same proclamation Jesus forgave the man's sin and healed him of his sickness.

James also tied forgiveness and healing together. Notice how he confidently asserts the outcome of prayers for the sick:

> *Is anyone among you sick? Let him call for the elders of the church, and let them pray over him, anointing him with oil in the name of the Lord. And the prayer of faith will save the sick, and the Lord will raise him up. And if he has committed sins, he will be forgiven. Confess your trespasses to one another, and pray for one another, that you may be healed. The effective, fervent prayer of a righteous man avails much.*
> JAS. 5:14-16

The Will of God and Healing

Although there is much debate over God's will toward healing, I hope to convince you that His will is not as mysterious as it seems. If you understand God's will toward salvation, you can understand His will toward healing, because the same principles apply to both. Failure to understand this connection has caused much confusion.

If you are a Christian, it's unlikely that you would need to ask the question, "Why are some people saved while others are not?" Most Christians know the answer to this question, which is found in the Bible:

> *The Lord is not slack concerning His promise, as some count slackness, but is longsuffering toward us, not willing that any should perish but that all should come to repentance.*
> 2 PET. 3:9

It is God's will that all people be saved. Men and women are saved by the preaching of the gospel. If the gospel is not preached, no one hears it. If they do not hear it, they are not saved (see Rom. 10:14-15).

Salvation comes when men and women cooperate with God in preaching the gospel and when they receive it. If men are not saved, it is not because God doesn't want them to be saved, but because man has not effectively preached the gospel or he has rejected it. The bottom line is – God's will about salvation is known. He wants all people to be saved, even if many are not.

The exact same principle applies to healing, because healing, like salvation, is an act of God's grace. Healing is delivered through believers like you and I. When we lay hands on the sick, God has an opportunity to heal them. If we fail to deliver healing or if people refuse to receive it, we shouldn't question God's will toward healing. Just as with salvation, His will is that we would be healed, even if not all people are healed.

God does not force His will upon anyone. He has chosen to limit the enforcement of His will so that we might be able to exercise free will. In addition, He has given key roles to non-human beings. We must account for the interactions of angels and demonic beings, which also have free will. God has limited His involvement in our affairs to the degree that He has allowed Satan and his minions to oppose virtually every aspect of His will – not only with regard to salvation, but with regard to healing.

Jesus healed all who came to Him. No one was turned away. As long as people were willing to be healed, He was willing to heal them. He didn't heal all who were sick, but rather, He healed all who were willing to be made well. Some who were sick, did not want to be healed, so they were not healed. The will of man is always honored by God, who gives to us according to our desires.

Some people argue that Jesus was looking for certain individuals whom the Father pointed out to him for healing, while avoiding others whom the Father did not want to heal. They believe that there were many people the Father did not want to heal for one reason or another. To support their assertion, they point to the fact that Jesus said He only did what He saw the Father doing (see Jn. 5:19).

The problem with this view is that in numerous accounts in the gospels, Jesus visited villages and it was said that He "healed them all." Rather than looking for certain people to heal while avoiding others, He healed everyone who wanted to be healed – without exception. It seems more likely that what Jesus referred to when He said He only did what He saw the Father doing – is that He was given instructions from the Father on *how* to heal each person, rather than *which* person to heal.

If there were no exceptions to healing in the life of Jesus, there are no exceptions to healing in the will of the Father. Bill Johnson observed that "Jesus is perfect theology." Any belief we have about God that we don't see modeled in the life of Jesus should be carefully considered and probably rejected.

If the will of God was for us to be sick, then no one disregarded the will of God more than Jesus. Every time He healed someone, He may have cheated them of a lesson they needed to develop their character. You could argue that persecution builds character, because the Bible teaches that Godly character comes by enduring persecution (see 1 Pet. 4:12-19). But you can't argue from Scripture that sickness builds character. Nowhere is this taught in the Bible.

It seems more likely that what the Father showed Jesus wasn't who could or could not be healed, but how they should be healed. While Jesus healed all who came to him – He used a different method nearly every time. It was probably the method and not the individual that the Father showed Him. Later in the book we'll describe the various methods used in healing and how we can receive instruction from the Father on which method to use and when.

The Will of the Enemy

We must also consider the will of the enemy with regard to healing. Jesus said the enemy comes to steal, kill and destroy (see Jn. 10:10). In calling His enemy a thief, He revealed that Satan's activities are illegal. The fact that stealing is illegal doesn't keep people from committing robbery. God allows crime, not because He approves of it, but because He values free will and wants us to exercise our free will partnering with Him in abolishing lawlessness. In the same way, God allows sickness not because He approves of it, but because He values free will and wants our participation in His plan to defeat it. Sickness is now an unauthorized activity carried out by the kingdom of darkness.

There are criminals who break the law and there are agents authorized to fight illegal activity. In the same way that police fight crime, we are commissioned to fight sickness. Healing is a matter of enforcing God's will here upon the earth as His representatives.

Ephesians chapter six teaches that we are involved in a war against the enemy and Psalm 84:11 says that God withholds no good thing from us. Bearing these things in mind, let's look at a passage that will help clear up the issue of God's timing and healing:

> *And when they had come to the multitude, a man came to Him, kneeling down to Him and saying, "Lord, have mercy on my son, for he is an epileptic and suffers severely; for he often falls into the fire and often into the water. So I brought him to Your disciples, but they could not cure him."*

> *Then Jesus answered and said, "O faithless and perverse generation, how long shall I be with you? How long shall I bear with you? Bring him here to Me." And Jesus rebuked the demon, and it came out of him; and the child was cured from that very hour.*
> MT. 17:14-17

After repeated failed attempts by the disciples to heal his son, the man could have easily concluded that it wasn't God's will for his son to be healed or that it wasn't God's time. Failure robs us of hope and hope deferred makes the heart sick. But this man didn't give up hope – he went to Jesus.

By casting out the demon and healing the boy, Jesus demonstrated that the condition (epilepsy) had a spiritual cause and that it was God's will and time for the boy to be healed. Many well-meaning people will attempt to heal the sick and fail, because they haven't developed faith that consistently heals. We can't fault them for trying, but we shouldn't assume that their failure means that God doesn't want healing to take place. Failed healing usually results from a lack of faith on the part of the healer, not a lack of willingness on the part of God. Remember, Jesus rebuked His disciples for their lack of faith when the boy was not healed. If someone has prayed with you and you haven't been healed, don't let their failure make you believe that God doesn't want you healed. Be like the Father of the sick boy and find someone full of faith or go to Jesus yourself.

Healing is sometimes a gradual process, like the rest of God's work in our lives. From the first day we believe in Christ as our savior, changes begin to take place. Although we are immediately given the righteousness of God, our conduct doesn't immediately become righteous. The transformation from rebellious sinner to obedient son or daughter is a process called sanctification. How quickly it happens is determined by our cooperation with God. The more we resist, the longer it takes. Over time, God's grace transforms us into the image of His Son.

Salvation, though it is immediately available, may take time to be brought to fulfillment. Healing can be much the same way. God's grace for healing is always available. We can obtain it immediately. But the change in our body may take time. God's plan for healing can be resisted by us and by the enemy, slowing our healing. In another chapter we'll look at the ways that we can work against God's plan for our healing.

Most of the people I know who operate in healing have something they want to be healed of. I've been healed of neck and shoulder pain, back pain, and a heart condition that I had for 25 years. But I'm still waiting for my eyes to be healed. I believe my healing is coming, so I've decided to wait for it. I think it's worth our time to pursue healing with a passion. But until it arrives, we must patiently wait.

Ken's Dream

In most of the chapters of this book, I'll share my own revelation from God in the form of dreams, but in this chapter our dream comes from a friend. Ken Nichols has been used by God in healing for some time. He wrestled with the question of whether he had blanket authority to pray with everyone for healing or if he had limited authority to pray only for certain people. On December 5th, 2010, Jesus paid him a visit in a dream and answered that question. This is his account:

Before I explain the dream, let me give some background. Now as many of you may know I fully realize from the Word of God, that we are one with Christ who has been given all authority in Heaven and earth. Jesus our example and teacher demonstrated to us the will of the Father in all things, including healing the sick. He never prayed for even one, instead He gave a word of command and declaration. Another way of saying this is, He exercised authority and healed them. But there have been some books I read and those who are well meaning who said: "We only have authority over those things we are specifically given authority over, it's not just a blanket authority!"

I had been looking in the Word of God to see where Jesus ever said He lacked authority to heal someone, where He said He lacked the authority to do a miracle or stop a storm. Instead we see Him even "cursing" a fig tree and it dried up from the roots. So did Father God tell Jesus to curse the tree, thus giving Him specific authority? I think not. Same as with Elijah when the captain and his 50 men showed up on three occasions and he called fire down on them and burned them up. On the third time an angel was sent to tell Elijah not to fear them and go with them. So if God had to give specific authority to the prophet or nothing would happen, the angel would not have needed to be sent, to stop him from burning them up too. Authority means just that; pre-permission to do what had already been spoken for you to do. Jesus said heal the sick, cast out devils, raise the dead, etc.

Anyway, in the dream I had, I was sitting in an empty room on a chair and was praying and asking Jesus about this teaching. In the room there were couches and other chairs around a table. I had my head slightly down and facing straight ahead, as I was praying and asking for clarity, Jesus walked in the room off to my side. I felt His presence; I heard His voice and the atmosphere shifted. He physically walked in, not some spiritualized visitation. He said: "I hereby give you specific authority to heal all the sick, infirm and hurting. That clears that up! I want all of them healed, but you will never be able to reach all of them, so whoever YOU choose to minister to, I not only want them healed, I expect them to be healed. I will be there and watching what you do and how determined you are to see them made well. Once you decide to minister to this one or that one, you have a responsibility to their healing, unless they choose to walk away from it." (What came to my mind in the dream was similar to what John G. Lake had his Divine Healing Technicians do for graduation from his training. He gave them a name of someone in the community – typically terminal or incurable and told them to go and heal them and come back. If you don't heal them, don't come back.) Jesus then said, "You now have specific authority right from me and you never have to wonder or question that again. But with it comes responsibility as well. If you give up, if you try and fail I want you to come back here and we'll talk. I want all of them healed, remember that." Then the dream ended.

Ken goes on to say that rather than trying to find certain people to heal, he was left with a sense of the extreme love that Jesus has for all people and His desire to see all of them healed.

CHAPTER THREE

Identity

WHEN JESUS WALKED THE STREETS of Galilee, His acts of healing created division among those who watched Him. Some rejoiced at the miracles they witnessed, while others criticized Him. The same attitudes exist today. Healing, deliverance and miracles are ways in which the kingdom of God is made manifest through us. When we bring the kingdom of God to earth, we invite criticism, because wherever the kingdom goes, it destroys belief systems that are opposed it.

The greatest criticism of healing during the first century came from religious leaders. They had followers who admired their shallow spirituality. The miracles of Jesus drew people away from them and turned their hearts back to God. The kingdoms these men had built were beginning to crumble. Their response was to criticize the new thing God was doing. Little has changed today. Most of the criticism of healing today comes from religious leaders who are building their own kingdoms.

When you begin to heal the sick, and you do it in a setting where healing is not widely accepted, don't be surprised if church leaders oppose you. I know a few pastors who embrace healing, but many do not. For example, when I was new to healing, my pastor Dennis Teague encouraged me to pursue it. He set aside a time for healing every Sunday during church services. In contrast, I have received reports from many Facebook friends who were asked not to come back to their churches after they began healing the sick. I believe some of this is due to attitudes of stubbornness and fear. Leaders can be intimidated when their followers are doing things they aren't doing.

To have success in healing, you must deal with the issue of what people think of you. If you have fear of what others think of you, it may prevent you from realizing your full potential. You must learn to put aside the criticism of co-workers, church leaders, family and friends. Jesus wasn't popular with religious leaders or his family. He was despised by many people, but the sick loved Him like crazy because to them, He was the "fragrance of life." And I believe that kind of life is worth pursuing.

When I became interested in healing, I noticed something in the gospels that I'd never spent much time thinking about. Jesus healed a lot of people. If you don't think healing is for today or you don't think it's your calling, it's easy to overlook just how many people He healed. As I studied His life, I realized that there wasn't much else He did that could be called "ministry." He taught in the synagogues and preached the kingdom as people followed Him. But He spent an enormous amount of time healing the sick. The more I studied His life, the more I knew there was something missing from mine.

The Bible reveals many things about us. When we read it we tend to identify with someone. I might see the heart of King David and identify with him. You might see yourself in Deborah or Ruth. Some identify with the apostle Paul. We all see someone whose life is similar to our own. But almost no one looks at Jesus and says, "I can see myself in Him."

The people we strongly identify with become our role models. Ironically, we aren't called to become like the apostles or prophets. God's plan is for each of us to be conformed into the image of Christ. If we never identify with Jesus, we have a big problem. God wants us to become like Him and that means He must become our role model. But many of us have used a pastor or one of the disciples as a role model instead. If we are to be transformed into His image, we must begin to identify ourselves with Him. He must become our model in everything we do. We must allow Him to live His life through us.

A Change of Mind

The first message Jesus preached was, "Repent! For the kingdom of Heaven is at hand" (see Matt. 4:17).

The message of repentance has become well-known, even among those who are not religious. But its true meaning has become distorted over the years. The word repent, which is used in most English bible translations, comes from the Latin translation of scripture. It implies a change of action in an attempt to gain favor with someone.

The Greek word used in this passage is the word *metanoia*, which comes from two words; one refers to a change; the other refers to the mind. The instruction of Jesus was not for people to change their behavior to gain favor with God. He wanted them to change their way of thinking, because the kingdom of God had arrived.

For centuries, people tried in vain to please God by following religious laws. Their idea of repentance was to conform their outward behavior to the law, in order to please God. Jesus was approached by many people who believed they had kept the law perfectly. He said that no matter what they did, they could not keep the law, because the law dealt not only with external behavior, but with the thoughts of the heart, which are harder to control.

Jesus changed the emphasis and tone of the spiritual conversation. Rather than focus on keeping the law by our own strength of will, He emphasized the love that the Father has for us. He taught and demonstrated through His life and death that the Father loves us more than we can ever comprehend. The good news of the gospel is that God is in love with you. It is only when the heart is gripped by the affection of the Father that our outward behavior begins to change in a real way.

When I became a Christian, I listened to preachers who drilled into my head the idea that God saw me as a worthless sinner. I was taught that He really didn't like me very much, but He decided to save me, despite my wretchedness. I accepted this view of myself and after a while the word "sinner" became my identity. After years of living a powerless, defeated life, God said He didn't see me that way. He said that my true identity was a beloved and cherished son – not a worthless sinner.

On June 25, 2012, I had a dream that revealed something important about identities.

In the dream, I was walking along a street and kept finding people who were lost and emotionally disturbed. They'd lost all sense of their identity. As I talked with them, it was revealed to me what their true identity was. I reminded them of who they were and their identities were restored.

The more you accept God's love for you personally – the more your identity as His child will be established. And the more your identity as His child is established, (and your false identity is removed) the greater the power of His kingdom will become manifest through you. Manifesting the miraculous power of God is a matter of understanding and accepting your identity in Christ.

Through many different dreams, God began to show me things that I would do which seemed impossible. He showed me how I would affect people's lives around the globe. His plans for me were so much greater than the ones I had for myself. Rather than a life of mediocrity, He showed me the inheritance we have as heirs of His kingdom. As sons of God, we have truly been given exceedingly great promises.

Many of us are afraid of becoming prideful. In an attempt to remain humble, we prefer to see ourselves as less than how God sees us. When we see ourselves this way, we destroy the work He wants to do in and through us. True humility isn't thinking less of yourself. It's thinking of yourself exactly the way God thinks of you; not more and not less.

The key to operating in the power of God is in knowing your identity in Christ and knowing how He wants to work in you. You must shed the false identities you've accepted from man and receive the identity given to you by God.

CHAPTER FOUR

Dreams and Visions

THIS BOOK IS DIFFERENT FROM other books on healing. Most authors rely solely on the Bible and their personal experiences to teach on the subject of healing. God has taught me many things about healing through dreams and visions, so I will teach from the Bible and my experiences, but I'll *also* share some of the dreams I've had. I'll include an overview of dreams and visions from a biblical perspective in order to give you a better understanding of their relevance.

Even thousands of years ago, men understood how God uses dreams. Job's friend Elihu reminded him that because we often fail to perceive God's voice while we're awake, He reveals secrets to us while we sleep:

> *"For God may speak in one way, or in another, yet man does not perceive it. In a dream, in a vision of the night, when deep sleep falls upon men, while slumbering on their beds, then He opens*

> *the ears of men, and seals their instruction. In order to turn man*
> *from his deed, and conceal pride from man, He keeps back his*
> *soul from the pit, and his life from perishing by the sword."*
> JOB 33:14-18

Daniel and Joseph were skilled in dream interpretation. Because of it, they were promoted to positions of great power under the rulers of their respective lands. They both said that dreams and their interpretations came from God (see Gen. 40:8 and Dan. 2:28).

The Bible says, "It's the glory of God to conceal a matter, and the glory of kings to search a matter out." (See Prov. 25:2.) God conceals His plans in symbolic language to draw us into a closer relationship with Him. The Bible is full of accounts where God revealed important things through dreams. Here are a few examples:

In Genesis 31, Jacob had a dream in which an angel told him that God knew how Laban had cheated him over the years. The angel told him to leave Laban's land secretly. Laban was also warned by God in a dream not to speak harshly to Jacob about it.

Abimelech was warned in a dream not to sleep with Abraham's wife or he would die (see Gen. 20:3).

Joseph's cell-mates had divine dreams; one of them was promised freedom; the other was warned of his impending death (see Gen. 40:5).

Pharaoh was warned in a dream about a coming famine that would last seven years (see Gen. 41).

When Joseph learned that his wife Mary was pregnant, he considered leaving her, but an angel came to him in a dream and revealed that her pregnancy was a divine miracle and that he was to fulfill his marriage commitment. He was also warned in a dream of Herod's plan to kill Jesus and he was told to flee to Egypt. The accounts are recorded in Matthew chapters 1 & 2.

In Genesis 28, Jacob fell asleep by a river. God came to him in a dream and gave him several covenant promises: to bless him all of his days, to make a great family for him, to give him the land promised to Isaac and Abraham, and that all the nations of the world would be blessed through him.

God appeared to Solomon in a dream while he slept, telling him to ask for anything he wanted. In the conversation, Solomon asked for wisdom to rule over God's people. God gave him wisdom greater than anyone who ever lived. He also received great honor, riches and a promise of long life if he would be obedient. When Solomon woke up he realized all these things happened while he was sleeping (see 1 Kgs. 3:5-15).

Gideon was told to spy on his enemies before a battle. He discovered that one of them had been given a dream of a loaf of bread rolling down a hill, which smashed their tents. The enemies interpreted the dream as a sure sign of defeat. Gideon went back to his camp and confidently led his troops to victory (see Jud. 7:13-15).

King Nebuchadnezzar was given a dream concerning his own kingdom and all the kingdoms to follow. It was revealed that his kingdom was the greatest of the kingdoms of man. He was greatly encouraged by this dream (see Dan. 2:36-45).

God also uses visions to reveal His plans to us. He spoke to Aaron and Miriam about the way in which He would communicate to His prophets:

> *"If there is a prophet among you, I the LORD, make Myself known to him in a vision; I speak to him in a dream, not so, with my servant Moses, who is faithful in all my house, with him I speak face to face, even plainly, not in dark sayings."*
> NUM. 12:6-8

Both the apostles Peter and Paul were given assignments from God in visions. Dreams and visions are very similar; the main difference is that visions occur while we are a wake. In his vision, Paul saw a man from Macedonia praying. God told Paul and his friends to go there. Peter had a series of visions (actually described as a trance) in which God showed him (symbolically) that the 'unclean' Gentiles he disliked were the ones God wanted him to reach next with the gospel (see Acts 10:9-15 and 16:9-10).

When the prophet Samuel anointed Saul as the first king of Israel, he knew in advance all the details of the encounter. He knew where Saul would go after he left and all the people he would meet. It's likely that God revealed some of this information to Samuel through dreams or visions (see 1 Sam. chapters 9 and 10).

Both Daniel and the apostle John saw events that would take place thousands of years in the future; all of them were revealed through dreams and visions. Here are two examples of what God has done through dreams and visions in modern times:

Charles Spurgeon, the famous 19th century preacher was given an entire sermon in a dream. His wife wrote it down and he preached it to the congregation the following Sunday.

The city of Spokane, Washington was once called the healthiest city in the world, due to the healing ministry of John G. Lake. He was a millionaire who held an influential seat on the Chicago Board of Trade. While in prayer one night he had a vision from God that lasted four hours. In the vision he was given all the details of the next season of his life. Later he moved to Indianapolis, then to South Africa, where he had an incredible ministry in healing and church-planting. Later he moved to Spokane, Washington and started the healing rooms there. Records show that over 100,000 people were healed there in a span of five years. All of these things were revealed to him in the night-vision.

As I mentioned in the introduction, since 2008, I've had hundreds of dreams and visions involving different aspects of healing. In some of them, I was praying with a person who needed healing and in others I watched healing miracles take place. Many of the dreams have been instructional; God taught me things about healing that I didn't know. Some of the dreams revealed things about healing that are not clearly explained in the Bible.

I don't believe our personal revelation has greater authority than Scripture. The word of God is our best place to turn for instruction. We should not accept anything that contradicts the clear teaching of Scripture. But the Bible does not exhaustively discuss the subject of healing. Instructional passages on healing are rare and some of the teachings of Jesus (particularly the kingdom parables) are highly symbolic. Because of this, there is a lot of ambiguity concerning the practice of healing.

Some people take the view that where Scripture is silent we should remain silent. Since I began having dreams from God about healing, I've realized that He wants us to know more than what is contained in the Bible. This is why He gives us dreams. The Holy Spirit is given to us as the Spirit of Truth, who leads us into all truth (see Jn. 16:13). As you read about the dreams God has given me, I'll ask you to discern if there is truth in them or not.

CHAPTER FIVE

Healing and Relationships

THE ADVICE IN THIS CHAPTER is largely that which I received from a trusted friend and mentor who goes by the name of Nor'west Prophetic. His observations have profoundly changed the way in which I minister healing to people and it's given me favor wherever I go.

I am sometimes asked, "Exactly how do you walk up to a complete stranger in a store and ask if they want to be healed?" Every person we meet is a stranger at first. Everything we do from the time we meet them either builds or destroys the relationship. If we want to heal a stranger, at minimum we should probably learn their name. (Personally I think we should go much further, but it's a start.)

There are many ways to approach strangers – some are better than others. You could stand on a sidewalk with a loudspeaker announcing your desire to heal people, commanding them to be healed from ten feet away. You might even heal a few of them. But I don't think it would qualify as effective ministry. Most of us want to know something about the one representing God before we give them our time and our ear. When a stranger speaks at a church, they're introduced and their credentials are presented. It's part of our culture.

A few years ago I met Nor'west Prophetic through a website he authored. I liked the things he wrote so much that I began corresponding with him by e-mail. He was very gracious and patiently answered some of my questions and encouraged me to find the rest of the answers on my own. We became good friends and over time, I realized that he saw me more as a peer than as a student. One day I wrote something that provoked him to thought. Here is the inspiring response he sent me:

> Some time ago, I had an image of a network of islands in a vast sea, connected by a variety of bridges. The islands are people, and the bridges are the relationships. Some of the islands have many bridges, some just a few, and a few islands have no bridges at all. And the bridges are of all varieties. There are some rickety footbridges, some rope bridges or narrow wooden bridges. Some are just a fallen log. Others are well-made stone bridges, and there are a few modern steel or concrete bridges.

> "No man is an island," or so John Donne says. Nobody is completely self-sufficient. I may produce quite a lot of what I need on my island, but there are some things that I'll need from others. Besides, if I get by with only what I can make myself, then I subject myself to a very primitive lifestyle: no cars, no cell-phones, no laptops or toilet paper: none of these can be produced without heavy industry. If I want coffee, I can trade some of the things I make on my island (let's imagine I'm a carpenter) with someone else for their coffee, but only if I have a bridge. But not just any bridge. I need to have a bridge that I can carry my wood furniture over: the rope bridge won't do. In fact, the fallen log is out, and many of the narrow wooden bridges. The guy with the coffee can make use of most of the bridges, but my work requires a bigger bridge. The stonemason on the next island over needs really strong bridges.

> I heard Rick Joyner say one time that when God sends him somewhere to minister, he's always interested to see how they receive him. If they recognize him as a pastor or ministry leader, then there's a certain amount of ministry

he can bring. If they receive him as an author and a teacher, then there's more he can bring. If they can accept him as a prophet, still more, and if they welcome him as an apostle, then he can bring the entire arsenal for them. Rick is looking to see what kind of bridge exists between himself and the people he's ministering to. If it's a smaller bridge, built with less trust or less understanding of the things of God, then he's able to bring less ministry over the bridge, perhaps just the ministry of a pastor. After a number of visits, perhaps the bridge is strong enough to support apostolic ministry.

If I don't have any relationship with you at all, then it will be very difficult for me to minister to you, to strengthen you, encourage you, to equip you for the assignments that God has given you. Likewise, it's nearly impossible for *me* to receive any strength or encouragement from *you*. There are people I know professionally; most of them don't have a bridge with me that would support a prophetic word or a revelation from Scripture.

When I speak with a group of people, the first thing on my agenda is to build relationship with them. I only have a few minutes with them, maybe an hour, so we have to work fast; I do that work with jokes, stories, and illustrations. Fortunately, I have a teaching gift from God and the Holy Spirit loves to inhabit them: He makes the job much easier and faster, but it still takes time, and if I hope to carry something of value to them, I must have a bridge to do it! Even Jesus saved His heavy revelation for the Last Supper, after Judas had left to collect his 30 pieces of silver. Only there among His eleven most trusted friends did He share his most significant secrets. Those were the only relationships that were able to bear it.

For a more scriptural example, let's look at 1 Corinthians 3. It's my opinion that this is essentially what Paul is saying: "Your end of the bridge isn't substantial enough for this ministry." They were acting like "mere men" which prevented him from teaching them weightier subjects. Same with Hebrews 5. The seven sons of Sceva may be an example of the bridge of relationship breaking because they tried to carry too much weight over it, but Stephen certainly is such an example.

Recently, I needed to bring a very strong word of correction to a brother in Christ. I actually had the word two years earlier, but the word was heavy enough that our relationship couldn't support it. We built a relationship over those years, and eventually he invited me to speak into his life on that subject, and when I did, our relationship supported the weight of the word: he made the needed changes in his life (it took a few years) and we're still friends. Now we both speak into each other's lives.

Now the question is whether you and I have enough of a relationship to support this much meat? It's not really a lot of weight, but then, we don't have a lot of experience relating to each other either.

I thought about my friend's words for a long time. Then I thought about people I've met who can't receive advice or correction from leaders, because they've never had a relationship with a leader that was strong enough. Some go from church to church, unfortunately unable to receive correction from anyone. Many pastors never get to know their congregations well enough to give advice without causing offense or intimidation.

I thought about the sidewalk evangelist who brazenly walks through town condemning people to hell, without ever stopping to ask their name or demonstrate one act of compassion toward them. I thought about street healers who go around healing injured people just to gather testimonies to share with anyone who will listen and leave without anything else being said to the one who was healed. And I came to this conclusion: ministry flows through relationships.

We must learn how to develop bridges of relationship with people if we hope to minister healing (or anything else) to them. Even if it's a small bridge, they must have a reason to trust us. Healing may just be the beginning of their life in the kingdom. After healing or deliverance they'll need to be discipled. Who does that? It might be us if we have the relationship to support it. We need an approach to ministry that is relational. Where do we find a relational model of ministry?

When I'm looking for an example of effective ministry, I think about how Jesus did things. He healed people in a variety of ways. Sometimes the sick came to Him. Sometimes a family member sought His help. He didn't need to establish who He was in those cases. They knew He had the power to heal and they trusted Him. All He did was release the healing to them. But sometimes He healed strangers who knew nothing about Him. How did He gain their trust?

My favorite example is when He met the woman at the well of Samaria as recorded in John chapter 4. Here's a brief overview of their encounter:

- Jesus departs from Judea and heads toward Galilee, passing through Samaria (verses 3-4).
- He meets a woman at the well and asks for a drink (verse 7).
- She is offended at His request (verse 9).
- They discuss the nature of water (verses 10-15).
- Jesus gives her a prophetic word about her current boyfriend and previous husbands (verses 17-18).
- She recognizes Him as a prophet (verse 19).
- They discuss religious practices (verses 20-24).
- She brings up the subject of the Messiah (verse 24).
- He reveals that He is the Messiah (verse 25).

Jesus took a perfect stranger and in a few minutes convinced her He was the Messiah. We don't need to convince people that we're the Messiah, our task is much easier. We just need to show them through kind words and actions that we care enough about them to have God bless them with His healing power.

My suggestion is simple. Take a few minutes. Get to know the person you want to see healed. If they have an obvious injury, ask how it happened. Ask about the weather or their children. Ask about anything you might have in common with them. If you see sadness, ask what it's about. If you sense fear, ask what they're afraid of. Listen to what they say and respond out of compassion.

Take time to establish a bridge of trust before attempting to minister to strangers. People don't care how much you know until they know how much you care.

CHAPTER SIX

Motives for Healing

IT'S POSSIBLE TO DO THE right thing for the wrong reason. Healing, which in itself is a good thing, can be done out of questionable motives. I've had to check my motives more often than I'd like. When I began this life of healing, it was at the prompting of God. He kept after this reluctant, unbelieving skeptic until I finally got in the flow and saw people healed. I'm glad He was more persistent than I was. As time went on, I stepped out and laid hands on the sick more often because it was finally working. People were actually being healed.

There came a day when I began to feel a bit guilty because no one had been healed and I was making my way to bed. I began to wonder if I was becoming lazy. Two days went by and I failed to lay hands on a single person. I began to wonder if God was disappointed with me. After a week of kicking back on my "no healing vacation" I wondered to myself, "If I laid hands on someone, would they actually be healed?"

65

My guilty conscience got the best of me and I went back to praying with people in stores again. And they were still being healed.

I decided to kick it into high gear for a while and started looking for people to heal literally everywhere I went. My wife began to get a little irritated. She could no longer have a normal conversation with me at a restaurant because I was always looking for someone who needed healing. It became a kind of obsession. I was turning into a healing machine with no "off" switch.

I had a talk with Jessie Campbell one night about my situation. Jessie operates powerfully in healing and teaches others as well. She lives in Australia, so we talked over Skype. I shared my concerns about having a guilty conscience over not healing people, then becoming compulsive about it. She told me she'd been through the same struggles. We talked for a long time about healing and the motives we have for doing it. I came away from that discussion with a clearer perspective. I'd like to share a few observations about our motives for healing.

Some of us are "doers" by nature. We love to keep busy, doing things to help others out. (I'm one of those types.) Healing lends itself well to this type of personality. But healing, like any form of ministry is supposed to be done out of compassion, not compulsion. The gospels often note that Jesus healed the multitudes because He saw them and had compassion on them, not because He had to heal 50 people a day to earn favor with His Father.

Jesus was a man who lived a balanced life. He was passionate about the things He did, but He operated in a great diversity of gifts. He was just as adept at healing and casting out demons as He was at teaching children. He preached in the synagogue one day and the next day He couldn't be found, having retired to the solitude of the mountains. He was just as comfortable in a fishing boat as He was with the nobles or the prostitutes. He shared the mysteries of the kingdom with thousands if they'd listen, but He was equally delighted in sharing with His three closest friends; Peter, James and John. He was and is a man for all occasions who meets the needs of everyone. Healing is neither the exclusive, nor the primary need of most people. The needs of the world are many and healing is only one of them.

I love healing. It gives me a thrill to see the power of God fix what the enemy has broken. The Church has been locked up in her tower long enough. I'm glad to see us hitting the streets and doing the things Jesus did. We ought to be healing the sick. But doing healing every day, all day long will eventually put you in a straight-jacket. There is more to life than healing. You don't need to look very far to find people whose lives have been ruined by the cruel taskmaster of compulsive healing.

I have healed some people out of a guilty conscience – thinking it was wrong to ignore anyone who needed healing. Please don't misunderstand me; healing is a good thing. Jesus told us to do it and everyone I've seen healed was grateful that I took the time to pray with them. But every good thing, if wrongly prioritized, can become an idol. It may even be bad for your mental health.

There is an explosion of healing taking place today in the body of Christ. Training is readily available for free. There are hundreds of YouTube videos available to teach you about healing. Many people will offer to train and lead you on the path to a successful healing ministry. You may be invited to join groups for study and practice. You'll make new friends in the healing community. You'll hear amazing testimonies about the power of God. But you'll also see great division over how healing is supposed to be done. And you'll eventually find those who will place enormous pressure on you to heal people every waking hour and accuse you of being lazy and disobedient if you don't. Their Jesus has a yoke that's hard and a burden that's heavy.

Anyone can heal the sick because they want to see the power of God at work. Brush aside the rhetoric and all you have is sorcery. Anyone can heal from a compulsion to obey the commands of Jesus; this person is no more than a legalist trying to be justified by his works. Anyone can heal so that they can tell their friends how God is using them. Such a man will be destroyed by his own pride.

Be cautious in developing relationships in the healing community and seek God's wisdom at all times. Don't be swayed by clever arguments or impressive testimonies from those who may recruit you to their group. Examine the fruit of their lives. Don't be taken by those who would place a yoke of bondage on you.

Go out and heal the sick, raise the dead, cast out demons and preach the kingdom. But do it for only one reason. Your motive should be an overwhelming love and compassion for those in need. There is no other legitimate motive for healing.

CHAPTER SEVEN

Faith for Healing

HEALING IS SOMETHING WE DO by faith. In contrast to traditional medicine, which is a function of what you know and how skilled you are, divine healing is a result of who you know and what you believe. Simply put, if you know Jesus and you believe He is still healing people today, He will heal the sick through you. Once your relationship with Him is established through the operation of the Holy Spirit, growing your faith in God's ability and desire to heal is the next step.

How do we develop the kind of faith that heals? Let's look at some of the reasons why people are not healed when we pray. The disciples of Jesus were not able to heal the boy with epilepsy and when they failed, they asked Jesus why:

And when they had come to the multitude, a man came to Him, kneeling down to Him and saying, "Lord, have mercy on my son, for he is an epileptic and suffers severely; for he often falls into the fire and often into the water. So I brought him to your disciples, but they could not cure him."

Then Jesus answered and said, "O faithless and perverse generation, how long shall I be with you? How long shall I bear with you? Bring him here to me." And Jesus rebuked the demon, and it came out of him; and the child was cured from that very hour.

Then the disciples came to Jesus privately and said, "Why could we not cast it out?"

So Jesus said to them, "Because of your unbelief; for assuredly, I say to you, if you have faith as a mustard seed, you will say to this mountain, 'Move from here to there,' and it will move; and nothing will be impossible for you."

MT. 17:14-20

We will discuss the connection between sickness and demons in the chapter on deliverance. In this chapter we will focus only on faith.

Jesus said the disciples could not heal the boy because they lacked faith. It appears as though they had adequate faith for healing some diseases, but not the faith required to accomplish this particular task.

Jesus said if they had faith as a mustard seed, they could move mountains. Some have taught that Jesus spoke of *size* when comparing faith to a mustard seed. They teach that just a small amount of faith can move mountains – if it is pure. I believe this teaching misses the point. Jesus didn't use *size* in this comparison. He didn't say they needed faith as *small* as a mustard seed, but rather they needed faith that *acts* as a mustard seed acts. It was the action, not the size, Jesus referred to. Small faith was never commended by Jesus. He often rebuked people for having little or small faith. He commended the Roman Centurion who had great or "large" faith (see Mt. 8:9-10).

In one of the kingdom parables Jesus likened the kingdom of God to a mustard seed, explaining that it grew into a large tree; so large that the birds of the air came to nest in it (see Mt. 13:31-32). Here is the key to how mustard seed faith acts – it grows. A seed bears no fruit until it germinates and grows into a plant; the larger the plant – the more fruit it bears. Faith that heals the sick may start out small, but it must grow before it produces fruit.

When I began praying for the sick, almost no one was healed. I became discouraged and I wanted to quit. I had almost no faith. All I had was a promise from God; "You pray and I'll heal." I had a seed of promise from God and nothing else. But as we've seen, the kingdom of God is about growth.

So I planted the seed and watered it. I watched videos featuring Todd White, Pete Cabrera and Tom Fischer as they prayed with people on the streets and I saw miracles happen. And the seed sprouted. I watered it with Scripture, reading every account of healing I could find in the Bible. And it grew roots. God gave me dreams where I saw myself praying for the sick and they were being healed. Leaves grew from a small stalk that emerged from the ground. I attended healing conferences and watched miracles happen before my eyes. I continued laying hands on anyone who would let me and eventually, I saw some of them healed. Fruit began to appear.

In the beginning, I failed to understand what it took to see people healed. I saw others operating consistently in healing and I wanted to know how they did it. Like many people, I misunderstood what faith for healing is and how it operates.

Most of you would call yourselves Christians, disciples of Jesus, or simply, "believers." You believe certain things about Jesus; the most important is that He is your Savior. This "kind" of faith is the kind that saves us from the consequences of sin, but it's not the kind of faith that heals the sick. Every Christian believes that Jesus is their savior, and yet that faith does not heal the sick. There must be another kind of faith that heals.

The kind of faith that heals isn't a belief that God wants to heal the sick. Many Christians believe that God wants to heal the sick and yet the sick are not healed when they pray for them. Faith that heals is different from this.

Faith that heals consistently and predictably is the belief (confidence) that when you are presented with an opportunity to heal someone who is willing to be healed, that God will in fact heal that person of the condition they have through you. Faith that heals consistently is not general. It is specific to the person who is sick, the problem at hand and the one who is praying. Allow me to illustrate:

When the woman was healed by taking hold of the hem of Jesus' garment, Jairus was in the crowd looking on. His daughter was sick and he came to Jesus for help. After the woman was healed, Jesus had her testify to the crowd. After she testified, a friend of Jairus appeared and informed him that his daughter had died. Jesus looked at Jairus and said, "Do not be afraid; only believe, and she will be made well" (see Lk. 8:40-50).

The woman's testimony was needed because Jesus wanted Jairus to hear it and have faith for something specific. Although believing that He is the Messiah is important, it wasn't the thing He was after. He didn't want Jairus to believe that God heals some people or that He raises some people from the dead. He wanted Jairus to believe without a doubt that *his* daughter would be raised from the dead. Notice that Jesus said the girl would be made well, *if* he believed. The faith Jairus needed to see his daughter resurrected was specific to his daughter and her condition. And this is the kind of faith we need for healing the sick.

When I began praying with people for healing, I seldom expected any of them to be healed. I believed that God wanted to heal some people and some conditions but I didn't believe He wanted to heal all of them and I thought the person I was praying with wouldn't be healed. I had a lot of doubts. Those doubts involved either the person I was praying with or the condition I was praying for.

I doubted that God wanted to heal everyone and in fact, I believed He would heal just about anyone except the person I was praying with. Because I didn't know that God wanted to heal everyone, my faith was generalized to *some* people, but not *specific* to the one I was praying with. So when I prayed with specific people, my doubts surfaced and I imagined them not being healed. My specific doubts destroyed my generalized faith and no one was healed.

After six months of fruitless attempts at healing, I realized I had to change some things. I noticed that Todd White commanded healing instead of asking God to heal and it worked well. Here's an issue we need to consider. Has it ever occurred to you that when we beg God for healing, we believe that we are more compassionate than He is?

I changed my approach and started to command healing and as soon as I did, I saw people healed – often they were healed instantly. I saw lots of success with torn rotator cuffs, as well as carpal tunnel syndrome. Seeing one person after another miraculously healed, it became easier to approach these two conditions with more confidence. After only a few more months I'd seen dozens of people healed with a success rate of around 90 percent. Because of that success, I began to believe (I had confidence) that God would actually heal everyone I prayed with who had one of these two conditions. My faith, which was generalized until then, became very specific. There were certain people with certain conditions that I knew in my heart, without any doubt God was going to heal. It was at this point that before praying with people, I told them they would be healed. Something had changed in my mind that led to greater confidence and better results. I'd like to explain how those changes occurred.

I began with a *generalized* faith about healing. My general belief was that God wanted to heal *some* people of *some* conditions. This faith was weakened by *specific* doubts. I doubted that God wanted to heal a *specific* person of a *specific* condition through *my* prayers.

Eventually, a few people were healed. As I saw more people healed, my generalized faith became specific. I had confidence (faith) that *some* of the people I prayed with would be healed, though not all. I had also more faith for some conditions than others. My doubt about specific conditions was also being removed. And my faith for just about every type of condition was greater than it had been.

As I began praying for people with neurological disorders like Parkinson's, multiple sclerosis, and ALS (Lou Gehrig's) I found that I had little faith. Over time, my confidence began to grow and I began to see changes in some of those people as well. The same is true for cancer. Like many of us, my confidence for seeing cancer healed was small.

I saw cancer as a stronger adversary, for some reason. But as I prayed with more cancer patients and saw some of them healed, my confidence for healing of cancer began to grow quickly. I don't yet have the same confidence for cancer or ALS that I do for joint injuries, but the more I lay hands on people with those conditions the more my faith grows.

My faith, like the faith of Jairus, was strengthened by watching the power of God at work. Faith can and must grow. Seeing people healed is one of the keys to growth. I don't think there is a substitute for witnessing the power of God at work.

The strategy for growing your faith is to start with a generalized belief that God heals. From there, you simply lay hands on whomever you can and eventually, you'll see some of them healed. As you do, your weak, generalized faith will become more specific and stronger. As you continue in healing, you'll see different types of diseases and injuries healed. You'll develop more faith for specific conditions. If you continue laying hands on people, the strong faith you have for a few things will broaden into a strong faith for many things.

There is a popular teaching that says some people have an "anointing" for healing certain conditions such as back pain or migraines. In reality, there is no specialized anointing. They've simply recognized the fact that they have greater confidence (or a lack of doubt) for some conditions than for others. If they continue to pray with faith for other conditions, they usually develop confidence for them as well.

Healing Amputees

It has often been noted (primarily by skeptics) that no one has produced a medically documented case of an amputee who has had a limb restored through prayer. They use this as an argument against healing. In light of all the other valid testimonies of healing it seems like a weak argument. But the question deserves to be answered, "Why aren't amputees healed in any significant numbers?"

I believe the lack of healing we've seen regarding amputees is due to nothing more than our corporate lack of faith *specific* to amputees.

We look at the amputee as an impossible assignment. Torn rotator cuff? No problem. Multiple sclerosis? Yes, we can do that. HIV? Sure, we've seen a lot of people healed of that. But when we face the man or woman with a missing limb, and we're asked to heal them, we don't have the faith (confidence) for it. When YOU believe (when you have a confident expectation) that God will heal a certain amputee through YOU, it will happen.

Great Faith

Jesus commented about the faith of the Roman centurion, calling his faith "great." I never considered myself to be a person of great faith. I thought that if I had great faith, every person I laid hands on who had missing limbs would have them grow out. I'd be able to walk on water and do many other signs and wonders if I had great faith. And since these things weren't happening, I concluded that my faith wasn't very great.

I had a dream one night about faith that changed my understanding of what it is and how it works. The dream was about a man who had great faith. His faith was so great that it could heal the entire city that he worked in. I didn't realize it at first, but understood later, that the man God showed me in the dream was me. What struck me most was the idea that it wasn't the man or even God that held the potential to heal all those people – it was the *faith* he had which held the capacity to heal an entire city.

In the dream, God revealed something I didn't know. He explained that my choice to continue praying with people, in spite of dismal results, was really the process of watering and nurturing the seed of faith that He gave me, which grew into faith that today has almost unlimited potential. I don't expect to heal an entire city, although that would be a great testimony to God. Such a feat would require me to stay awake for weeks or months on end and it would require that everyone in the city would *want* to be healed. God wasn't speaking about actual healing, but the *potential* to heal. He was saying that my faith had grown to the point where I had the potential to heal thousands, if I chose to operate in a way that tapped into the faith I now had.

We know that faith is the substance of things hoped for, the evidence of things not seen (see Heb. 11:1). Faith has substance. It's tangible and it does things, like heal the sick. I see faith as something like the currency of heaven. When we begin our journey in the kingdom, most of us have small faith. Our bank account of faith upon which we can draw out the resources of heaven is small. But as we walk with God and get to know His ways, we begin to trust Him more. As our faith in Him grows, so does the balance in our account. The more we step out and exercise our faith, the more we get to watch God at work. The more He works the more reason we have to trust Him. And trusting Him brings more faith into our account.

Unlike the balance in our bank account, which decreases the more we use it, the balance in our faith account increases the more we use it. Those who have great faith are those who exercise it often. Many of us underestimate what is possible with the faith we now possess. It's good to know that whatever level of faith we have today, it will increase if we exercise it.

The Gift of Faith

One of the gifts of the Holy Spirit is the gift of faith (see 1 Cor. 12:9). The gift of faith is like a deposit into our faith account. When God wants to accomplish something through us that we don't have enough faith for, He makes a deposit of faith into our account and with the sudden increase in faith, His will can now be accomplished.

Jesus healed people who had different levels of faith. Let's look at some healing encounters and discuss how faith works.

The Roman centurion had great faith, which Jesus commended. But the centurion wasn't the one being healed; he came on behalf of his servant. The servant was healed, though he may have been unaware that the centurion had asked for his healing (see Mt. 8:13).

In Mark chapter 9, the Lord delivered a boy with a mute spirit whom the disciples couldn't heal. Two things are worth noting here; Jesus rebuked the disciples for their lack of faith (verse 19) and the father admitted he also had little faith (verse 24). In spite of this, Jesus cast the spirit out. It's apparent that no one except Jesus had the faith required to remove the spirit or heal the boy.

In a third account, a woman with chronic bleeding pursued Jesus in a crowd. She grabbed onto the hem of His garment and power flowed out of Him, which healed her. He recognized that power had left Him and said that it was her faith that healed her (see Mt. 9:20).

In Matthew chapter 20, we read that Jesus found two blind men who cried out for Him when they knew He was approaching. He asked what they wanted. When they asked to have their sight restored, He healed them (see Mt. 20:30-33).

In the fourth chapter of Luke, Jesus cast a spirit out of a man without making any comments except that He commanded the spirit to be silent (verse 35). At the bedside of Peter's mother, Jesus rebuked her fever and it left. He then healed a multitude of people by laying hands on them (verses 39-40).

In looking at this sample of healings, we see some principles emerge. In some cases, the faith of the healer was the key, and in others, the faith of the sick person was the key element to healing. The healing of the woman with chronic bleeding required faith on her part. She knew that Jesus had the power to heal. Convinced that she would be healed if she just touched His garment, she pursued Him. The faith of the healer is not involved in this type of healing. It's a matter of God honoring the faith of the person in need. We may run into situations like this, but it's likely we won't be aware of them until after the healing happens, because we're merely acting as a conduit of God's power.

In contrast, other examples show that as healers we are expected to have faith for healing. The faith of the one who needs healing isn't important in these cases. What matters is *our* faith. When faith goes into action, the power of God is released and healing occurs. As our faith for healing grows, we can expect to see more consistent healing and more miracles. Once we have sufficient faith, Atheists, Muslims, Buddhists, and people of any religion or world-view can be healed with equal success.

CHAPTER EIGHT

Power and Authority for Healing

MOST OF US HAVE BEEN taught that healing comes when we ask God to heal someone who is sick or injured. We pray and God hears our prayer and based on His knowledge of the situation He decides to either heal them or not. If this is how you believe healing takes place, I would ask you to set aside your beliefs for a while as we examine what the Bible teaches about the process of healing.

Most of us were taught how to pray by someone we respected. That first prayer may have sounded something like, "God, please bless mommy and daddy and our dog, Buster... in Jesus name I pray, Amen!"

When we became older, our style of prayer probably changed. Some of us developed a bit more desperation; "God I really need this job! You know how much this means to me, so please hear me and make this job happen *now*... in Jesus name I pray, Amen!"

Some of us believe there is virtue in accepting the outcome of a situation, regardless of how it works out. "Lord, if it's your will, please heal grandma of cancer, but if it's not your will, give us the grace to accept her sickness and death."

I don't mean to be critical of those who offer such prayers in earnest. But most of us who pray this way seldom see people healed. After trying this approach and praying with hundreds of people but seeing almost complete failure, I discovered a better, more biblical approach. I suppose there's nothing more insulting than to be told we don't know what we're doing when we pray. As people of faith, we pride ourselves on our prayer life. But we should ask ourselves if our prayers for healing are effective or not.

Over the last year, I would estimate that about 80 percent of the people I have prayed with have been healed. In a week when my faith was operating consistently, about half of them were healed instantly. In a typical week I might pray with as few as ten or as many as 30 people for healing of different conditions. Occasionally, in a particular week, everyone I prayed with was healed. You must understand that this kind of success is not guaranteed and my results from week to week may vary greatly. I have some weeks, where the success rate may be closer to 30 percent, but that happens only rarely. A number of friends have reported a 100 percent healing rate for a particular weekend of ministry. The success we have is the result of using a different approach to prayer .

At this point, you may be wondering why we aren't setting up camp at cancer clinics if we have this kind of success. Unfortunately, it's incredibly difficult to find anyone in health care who will take you seriously when your specialty is faith healing. Supernatural healing is not yet accepted as a valid form of treatment by most hospitals and clinics. Even when hospitals employ chaplains, they don't expect them to work miracles. Their role is primarily emotional support and grief counseling. (I'll discuss divine healing in the setting of health care in more depth in a later chapter.)

On September 2, 2010, I had a dream in which I was standing on the edge of eternity with a group of friends who operate in healing. Pete Cabrera and Jessie Campbell were two of the people with me. While

I gazed into eternity, Jessie approached and handed me a scroll. I knew what was written on it. It had a declaration that said, "You have been given authority over all the power of the enemy." I took the scroll and wrote the words down. Then I approached another person and read the declaration to him and he wrote it down.

The dream was a revelation of an eternal promise given to those who want to heal the sick. We know that some forms of sickness are planned and carried out by the enemy. But we have been given authority over sickness, disease, trauma and all other powers of the enemy.

Largely due to the teaching of men like Andrew Wommack and Curry Blake, many believers have begun to see the kind of success in healing achieved by Jesus and His disciples. These believers have a confidence and tenacity you won't find elsewhere in the Church. They tend to function as a kind of spiritual police, arresting sickness and disease and enforcing the principles of God's kingdom.

The truth about healing will come as a shock to most Christians and it will challenge their theology. When you review the individual healing accounts recorded in the New Testament, you'll find that not once did Jesus or His disciples ask God the Father to heal a sick or demonized person. A few people begged Jesus for healing, but Jesus never asked His Father to heal them, nor did the disciples. That fact ought to make us reconsider how we approach healing. If it wasn't His approach to ask His Father to heal the sick, what approach did Jesus use? Let's have a look.

When Jesus was summoned by the Roman Centurion to heal his servant, the soldier recognized the authority He had over sickness. Here is one of the keys to healing – it's a matter of authority. Because the Centurion understood how authority works, his faith was able to apprehend healing for his servant. No prayer was involved; Jesus spoke a word and the servant was healed. It was a simple transaction involving the faith of the Centurion and the authority of Jesus. There are a number of other healings that occurred in this manner, recorded in Matthew chapter 8.

Although He used slightly different approaches in each encounter, Jesus usually spoke a word of healing, touched the sick person or in some way transferred power to them. He didn't ask His Father to heal them. A few passages from the New Testament when taken together reveal the plan Jesus had for His disciples in regard to healing and deliverance. It's actually a simple outline for operating in healing.

As recorded in Matthew chapter 10, Jesus chose twelve disciples and commissioned them to go out to the cities of Israel. These were His instructions to them:

> *"And as you go, preach, saying, 'The kingdom of heaven is at hand.' Heal the sick, cleanse the lepers, raise the dead, cast out demons."*
> MT. 10:7-8

He gave them authority over all the power of the enemy:

> *"Behold, I give you the authority to trample on serpents and scorpions, and over all the power of the enemy, and nothing shall by any means hurt you."*
> LK. 10:19

He revealed a few of the things His disciples would do:

> *"And these signs will follow those who believe: In My name they will cast out demons; they will speak with new tongues; they will take up serpents; and if they drink anything deadly, it will by no means hurt them; they will lay hands on the sick, and they will recover."*
> MK. 16:17-18

After He was resurrected He told them they would receive power:

> *"But you shall receive power when the Holy Spirit has come upon you; and you shall be witnesses to Me in Jerusalem, and in all Judea and Samaria, and to the end of the earth."*
> ACTS 1:8

He gave His disciples assignments for healing, deliverance and raising the dead, and He gave them the power and authority to do them. Now let's have a closer look at the kind of power and authority He gave His disciples.

Authority to Heal

Faith isn't the only factor involved in healing. Some healers have great faith, but lack an understanding of their authority. The word for "authority" which is found in Luke 10:19 is the Greek word, *exousia*. I looked up this word in *Strong's Concordance* and found the following definitions:

1. power of choice, liberty of doing as one pleases

2. the ability or strength with which one is endued, which he either possesses or exercises

3. the power of authority (influence) and of right (privilege)

Power to Heal

Faith and authority are two of the keys to healing, but there is a third key we must understand – power. Jesus gave power to His disciples. What kind of power did He give them? The Greek word translated "power" in Acts 1:8 is the word *dunamis*. *Strong's Concordance* gives the following definitions:

1. Strength, power, ability

2. Inherent power, or power residing in a thing by virtue of its nature, or which a person or thing exerts and puts forth

3. Power for performing miracles

The authority we have is the legal right to do the things Jesus commanded us to do. The power He gave us (the anointing) is the operation of the Holy Spirit in us. These definitions speak of power and authority that reside with the individual. While our authority is ultimately tied to the authority of Christ, it is given to us and it may be exercised by us in whatever way we choose. The power for healing is a manifestation of the kingdom of God that permanently resides in us. Once we've been given power and authority to heal the sick, we never need to ask God to do it. We have the power and authority to heal them ourselves. This power and authority is how Jesus and the disciples healed and it is no different for us today.

We've noted that some people were healed when power left Jesus as He passed by them. The woman healed of the bleeding disorder is one example. Some people feel heat or tingling sensations when I pray with them and some feel nothing at all. Yet many of them are healed, whether they feel anything or not. Some people feel power leaving their body when they pray for others, but I do not. The only thing I feel is the presence of God around me.

We must understand that the power to heal resides with us. It is true that the power does not originate in us. It comes from God. But it comes to us and is released through us by the power of the Holy Spirit operating in us. We are something like portable power stations walking the earth. How marvelous it is that He has placed His treasure in these very earthen vessels.

Before we close this chapter, I wanted to share one more point about authority. The Bible says that believers have been seated (past tense) with Christ in heavenly places (see Eph. 2:6). It also says that Christ is seated on a throne in heaven beside His Father (see Eph. 1:20). If we have been seated with Him, then we are also seated on a throne in heaven – which is *our* seat of authority. We rule and reign beside Him.

Rulers who reign from their throne do not engage their enemy directly in battle. They simply make declarations from their seat of authority and their declarations are carried out. It is the fact that they occupy a seat of established authority that allows their spoken commands to be carried out. It's not the individual, but the seat they occupy that grants authority. If they were not seated on a throne, their commands would not have the same effect. Once we understand how to occupy our seat of authority in heaven, and how to rule from it, everything we do takes on a different dimension. The exercise of our authority is not limited to healing. It extends to all areas of life.

Most of us have been taught incorrectly about prayer and healing. We haven't been informed about our power and authority. I don't want to be too critical of church leadership and this isn't meant to be a book on theology. But there are some erroneous things being taught in the Church that need to be corrected.

Many of us have cried out to God to do something for our loved one as they lay dying of cancer. God has already done all that He needs to do. He paid for their healing and He gave us the power and authority to heal them. The thief comes to our house to steal, kill and destroy the people we care about. If the tongue holds the power of life and death, then your mouth is a loaded gun, a weapon that destroys sickness and disease. Isn't it time you started using it? If you haven't begun to exercise this power and authority, there's no time like the present. Go ahead, step out of the boat and watch the power of God begin to work through you.

CHAPTER NINE

God's Healing Presence

HAVING LOOKED AT HEALING AS matter of faith, authority and power, we now turn to the presence of God and healing. I'll ask you to be patient with me as I share a few things in this chapter that you may not be familiar with. Some of the things we'll discuss might seem at first glance to be obvious contradictions in thought. But by the end of the chapter, I hope you'll see that the things which seem to be contradictions are not really contradictions, but a revelation of God's nature in a way you may not have considered before. I'll do my best to carefully explore the subject of God's presence and clarify misunderstandings before we're through.

After the day of Pentecost, when the Holy Spirit had been released and the disciples became filled with God's Spirit, they continued the healing model Jesus had given them. They became very adept at healing and casting out demons. Word of these miracles spread throughout the region and people began bringing their sick friends and relatives into the streets hoping they would be healed:

> *And believers were increasingly added to the Lord, multitudes of both men and women, so that they brought the sick out into the streets and laid them on beds and couches, that at least the shadow of Peter passing by might fall on some of them.*
> ACTS 5:14-15

This passage says that people brought out the sick hoping that the shadow of Peter might fall on them. The passage doesn't actually say that the sick were healed by Peter's shadow. It says that people *believed* his shadow had healing power. Why would they come to this conclusion?

We don't know for certain, but it seems as though the sick were healed as the disciples passed near them. We also know that on a few occasions, power went out from Jesus as He passed through a crowd and the sick were healed. The power (or anointing) upon Jesus flowed from Him to them. I believe the disciples carried the anointing of God just as Jesus did and when someone needed healing, power left them and the sick were healed, often without their knowledge. I believe the same thing is happening today.

Some of us carry the presence of God in a way that releases healing on a regular basis, often without our awareness and without a single word being said. I became aware of this phenomenon a few years ago, when some of my patients mysteriously began getting better during transports in the ambulance. Some of these transports were nothing short of miraculous.

On one transport, a comatose patient with very low blood pressure who was expected to die had an unexpected increase in blood pressure and came out of his coma before we got to the destination. I was so busy providing medical care that I didn't have time to pray for him. At first, I shrugged it off as wishful thinking, until the night I had a dream that revealed something I wasn't aware of.

In the dream, I transported a man who sustained crushing injuries in a car accident. I didn't provide any medical treatment or pray for him.

When we arrived at the hospital, the doctor asked what I did for him. I told him I didn't do anything, but I thought he was healed. And in fact, he was healed. In the dream, I knew that the presence of God had come into the ambulance and had healed all of his injuries, without my direct involvement. I just sat in my seat and did nothing. This dream was God's way of letting me know that He was in fact healing people through His presence, even though I wasn't always aware of it or directly involved in the process.

This begs the question: Why would God sovereignly heal someone that I didn't pray for, while other people I have prayed for did not appear to be healed?

First, there are many people I've prayed for who did not manifest healing while I was with them, but were later found to be completely healed. This isn't always the case, but it happens often enough to make me cautious about assuming someone wasn't healed.

In September of 2012, my wife and I traveled to Australia to teach on healing and deliverance. Part of our time was spent ministering to men and women who lived in shelters and hostels. One night we received a testimony from a man who was healed of a toothache as he stood next to me while I handed out sandwiches. No one prayed with him. He said he could feel a "presence" around us that he noticed as soon as we arrived.

Bill Johnson has seen many people healed by sovereign acts of God. There are many testimonies of people receiving their healing as they walked through the doorway of Bethel's prayer room, before receiving prayer. Johnson believes the sovereign acts of healing are God's way of leading us into greater things. What God does sovereignly, He does as an example for us. He wants us to pursue intentionally, what we see Him do sovereignly.

In 2011, I transported a man from one hospital to another hospital after his fingers were crushed in an industrial accident. When I picked him up he was in severe pain. While interviewing him I learned that he also had chronic back pain from bulging lumbar discs and that he was presently having pain in his lower back. I asked if he wanted to be healed of the pain in his back. I had a lot of faith for seeing back pain healed but much less faith for traumatic injuries, so I chose the one I had greater faith for as the starting point.

He said he wanted to be healed so I invited God's presence to come into the ambulance and I placed my hand on his left side. I shared with him the dream I had about God's presence healing the man in the ambulance and a couple of recent testimonies of healing. I didn't ask God to heal him or command his injuries to be healed. I just shared the stories with him and waited for God to make His move. A few minutes later he said, "You're freaking me out. The pain in my back is gone." After the pain in his back was healed, I commanded his heavily-bandaged fingers to be healed. Before we arrived at the hospital, the pain in his hand had subsided enough that he wanted to go to sleep. I was not able to see if his fingers were completely healed because of the bandages.

I often ask God to bring His presence into the room or ambulance while ministering healing. The concept of God's presence puzzles some people. A friend once asked, "If God lives in us, and we are one with Him then how can He also be apart from us?"

In order to answer this question, I'd like to do a brief survey from the Bible on the operation of the Holy Spirit and God's presence.

Some leaders teach that the Holy Spirit no longer rests "upon" God's people as He did in the Old Testament. They believe that as a result of the new birth, because the Holy Spirit lives *inside* of us, we no longer need the Holy Spirit to rest *upon* us. This would seem to make sense, but let's look at what the Bible says about how the Holy Spirit operates today.

In John chapter 14, Jesus taught the disciples about the relationship they would have with the Holy Spirit:

> "I will pray the Father, and He will give you another Helper, that He may abide with you forever – the Spirit of truth, whom the world cannot receive, because it neither sees Him nor knows Him; but you know Him, for He dwells with you and will be in you."
> JN. 14:16-17

Here we see two different relationships that believers can have with the Holy Spirit. He can dwell *with* us and *in* us. But there is a third relationship Jesus said they would have. In the first chapter of the book of Acts, He commissioned them, saying they would receive power when the Holy Spirit came *upon* (epi) them:

"But you shall receive power when the Holy Spirit has come upon you; and you shall be witnesses to Me in Jerusalem, and in all Judea and Samaria, and to the end of the earth."
ACTS 1:8

This third relationship with the Holy Spirit is noteworthy for a couple of reasons:

1. Jesus tied the power for ministry to the new relationship they had not yet experienced. "You will receive power – *when* the Spirit comes upon you."

2. When Jesus was baptized by John, the Holy Spirit came to rest 'upon' Him, and remained there (see Jn. 1:32). The baptism of Jesus was the point at which His ministry began. He received the anointing and power for ministry through the same experience He later told the disciples they would have.

In Acts 2:3, the Holy Spirit manifested as divided tongues of fire resting "upon" the believers. In Acts chapter 8, Peter and John went to Samaria to assist the new believers in receiving the Holy Spirit, as described in the following passage:

For as yet He had fallen upon (epi) *none of them. They had only been baptized in the name of the Lord Jesus.*
ACTS 8:16

The apostle Paul likewise assisted people in receiving the Holy Spirit after they became believers:

And when Paul had laid his hands upon them, the Holy Ghost came "on" (epi) them; and they spoke with tongues, and prophesied.
ACTS 19:6

Finally, Peter taught that the Spirit of God rested "upon" believers:

> *If you are reproached for the name of Christ, be happy; for the*
> *spirit of glory and of God rests "upon" (epi) you: on their part he*
> *is evil spoken of, but on your part he is glorified.*
> 1 PET. 4:14

The Bible teaches that the Holy Spirit does in fact rest "upon" believers today, just as He did with the saints of the Old Testament. If we agree that Jesus and the disciples had the Spirit come to rest *upon* them at the starting point of their ministry, we could make the case that the power for ministry depends on this experience.

In the account of creation in Genesis 1:2, we see the Spirit of God moving over the face of the waters. What this reveals is that the Spirit of God moves. We also know that the voice of God spoke as the Spirit was moving and things were created that had not yet existed. Implied here is the fact that when the voice of God speaks, when and where His Spirit is moving, creative miracles occur.

It is frequently taught that God is present everywhere and yet people claim that God's presence "shows up" in different locations for different reasons. How do we reconcile this apparent contradiction?

One of the main verses used to support the idea that God is present everywhere is from this observation by the psalmist:

> *Where can I go from Your Spirit?*
> *Or where can I flee from Your presence?*
> *If I ascend into heaven, You are there;*
> *If I make my bed in hell, behold, You are there.*
> *If I take the wings of the morning,*
> *And dwell in the uttermost parts of the sea,*
> *Even there Your hand shall lead me,*
> *And Your right hand shall hold me.*
> PSALM 139:7-10

This is where I must attempt to explain something that seems to be a contradiction. The Bible does teach (or at least it implies) that God is present everywhere. And yet it also teaches that in some way, He appears at certain times in certain places where He was not previously present, or at least not present in the same way. One example is when God's manifest presence (or His glory) inhabited the temple of worship. Another is the indwelling of His spirit inside of us, after we are born again. So here is our question – how can God become present in some place when He is already present everywhere?

Let's look at a few more passages of scripture.

In the following passage, God's Spirit appeared in a cloud, from which He spoke:

> *Then the Lord came down in the cloud, and spoke to him,* (Moses) *and took of the Spirit that was upon him, and placed the same upon the seventy elders; and it happened, when the Spirit rested upon them, that they prophesied, although they never did so again.*
> NUM. 11:25

In the days of the kings of Israel, the manifest presence (glory) of God rested between the cherubim, on the mercy seat, above the Ark of the testimony. At one point, Ezekiel witnessed the glory of the Lord as it departed from the temple:

> *So the cherubim lifted up their wings, with the wheels beside them, and the glory of the God of Israel was high above them. And the glory of the LORD went up from the midst of the city and stood on the mountain, which is on the east side of the city.*
> EZEK. 11: 22-23

The Holy Spirit is a person. He inhabits us and never leaves us. The manifest presence of God (His glory) is the spiritual substance of His being and not a person. God's glory (or presence) comes and goes, though His Spirit does not.

When people refer to God's presence being "everywhere" they're speaking of God's awareness of all that is happening in creation. But there is a different aspect to His presence, which is purely relational and it has to do with worship. It's this presence (His glory) that appeared in the temple. The presence of God as it was manifested in the temple, and which is now manifested at different times in different places, is not present everywhere or all the time. It is reserved for places and times of worship.

This aspect of His presence is manifested wherever the sincere worship of God takes place. It is there for the express purpose of entering into a relational experience with Him. God's glory brings healing, deliverance, creative miracles, and much more into existence. Wherever God's presence is manifested in this way, heaven touches earth.

God Was With Him

Jesus was fully God and fully man, but it wasn't His own divine power at work when He healed the sick. If the works that Jesus did were a result of His divinity, it would be impossible for us to do even one, because we are not God. The Bible says that Jesus emptied himself of His divinity and became a man just as we are (Phil. 2:6-8). The apostle Peter made the following comment about how Jesus was able to heal and cast out demons:

> *"God anointed Jesus of Nazareth with the Holy Ghost and with power: who went about doing good, and healing all that were oppressed of the devil; for God was with him."*
> ACTS 10:38

Peter's explanation was that Jesus didn't heal the sick because He was God, but rather, because He was anointed by God and that God was with Him.

Jesus is God and yet, the Bible teaches that God was with Him and that God's Spirit rested upon Him. Somehow, the oneness shared by the Godhead allows all these seemingly impossible relationships to exist, despite the fact that they seem to contradict one another. Since God's nature doesn't change and His nature has been to appear (manifest) as dwelling in people, resting upon them, and residing in certain places, His Spirit could rest upon you or I and His presence could manifest in a restaurant, your living room or my ambulance.

In October of 2011, I had a dream about God's presence that took place in a hospital. In the dream, I was talking with the hospital staff, introducing them to God's presence and praying for them to be healed. One of the patients was a baby about five months old. There was also a doctor who wanted healing for arthritis in his elbow and knee. But in the dream, I knew that healing wasn't the main goal. My primary goal was introducing them to the presence of God. Getting them healed was secondary.

If we want to have victory over sickness and we want people to recover faster with fewer complications, we should invite God's presence to come and make Him welcome when He arrives. God's presence can do the work of healing, deliverance and restoration that we need. I've read dozens of testimonies of people who were healed merely by resting in the presence of God in worship. Although healing is a tremendous blessing to those who receive it, the greater need we all have is to draw closer to God and to know Him in a deeper way. Healing is one way to bring people into a greater experience of His presence.

CHAPTER TEN

Freeing the Prisoners

WHEN YOU ASK STRANGERS IF they want to be healed, you will on occasion be turned down. I often wear my paramedic uniform because I'm either praying with people at work or on the way home from work. When in uniform, I rarely get turned down. But in street clothes, I get turned down more often. The funny thing is – some of the people who don't want me to pray for them are Christians. When they say no, they usually tell me about the church they go to and how many people are already praying for them.

I often meet people in wheelchairs who receive disability checks from the government. Some of them don't want to be healed. In most cases they fear that if they were healed, they would no longer receive money for their disability and they'd have to find a job. Not knowing if they could find work, they prefer to remain just as they are, because their income is guaranteed.

I've also met people with disabilities who refuse prayer because they refuse to believe that their disability reduces their quality of life. They tend to have an optimistic outlook on life. They don't believe their physical condition affects their happiness or productivity in any way. They're quick to dismiss the perception that they're less able than anyone else. These people rarely accept healing prayer, because they don't believe they need to be healed to have a better life.

I've decided not to engage people in debates about the value of healing. Jesus healed those who wanted to be healed. I think we should do the same. When I meet someone who doesn't want to be healed, I smile and continue looking for someone who does.

Being rejected can be discouraging, but I'm not as discouraged as I once was. I'm learning to accept the fact that some people are comfortable with their pain, sickness or whatever imprisons them. They've made a choice to keep their affliction and I must honor it. Apparently, God knew I was feeling a little rejected, so He gave me a dream to help illustrate one of the realities of how His kingdom works.

In the dream I was traveling to a variety of locations. My job was to facilitate the closure of prisons. People in the areas I traveled to had voted to close certain prisons and let the prisoners go free. My job was to make sure the prisons closed on time without any problems. I was a representative who had been given the authority to close them. Near the end of the dream, I went to one prison and asked if it was to be closed. I was told that I couldn't close that one yet, because the people had not yet voted to close it. This was the end of the dream.

I asked God to help me understand the dream. Here's what I heard Him say:

> The Spirit of the Lord GOD is upon Me,
> Because the LORD has anointed Me
> To preach good tidings to the poor;
> He has sent Me to heal the brokenhearted,
> To proclaim liberty to the captives,
> And the opening of the prison to those who are bound
>
> ISA. 61:1 (SEE ALSO LK. 4:18)

Many of us (myself included) have faulty beliefs about God and His sovereignty. In recent years, He has been speaking to me about freedom; specifically about our choices and His decision not to overrule them. As an evangelical Christian I was well-instructed about God's sovereignty – or so I thought. Back then, I was under the impression that God always does what He wants with little or no regard for what we want. I was taught to believe that He is all powerful, He calls the shots and we're subject to His sovereign will. I think this understanding of sovereignty is an oversimplification.

I believe that God is all-powerful; that is to say He has the ability and power to do anything He wants. But I believe He honors the free will of man much more than I've been comfortable with.

In my dream, a group of people had not yet voted to close a prison. Their decision was to keep it open and allow people to remain prisoners. And their decision had to be honored. Although God gave me authority as His representative to close some prisons and free the captives, this did not give me authority to overrule the free will of others. And this seems to be the main point God wants us to understand. It is His will that all of us would live free, but some of us have chosen to remain prisoners and His sovereignty does not negate our free will.

Some leaders teach that it is acceptable to cast demons out of people against their will. In studying the ministry of Jesus, I don't see this principle practiced or taught. I'm often surprised at how low-key and unobtrusive He was. He often simply asked, "What do you want from me?" In freeing those who were oppressed, He first inquired about their wishes, then gave according to what they asked for. He honored the desires and free will of others. He never used His authority to violate the free will of those who were in bondage.

Without question, we do have a great deal of authority in Christ. Using it properly seems to be the thing we struggle with. Perhaps the most common problem is not knowing the authority we have. The other problem is knowing our authority, but using it at a time when restraint might be the better thing. The harsh reality is that some people we desperately want to see healed, don't want to be healed and we must respect their wishes.

Most of us will be asked to pray for someone who truly doesn't want to be healed. Here's how this often happens: A well-meaning relative sends out a prayer request on behalf of someone with a severe illness. A number of people attempt to get them healed but the person dies a short time later. They conclude that it wasn't God's will for them to be healed. What they often overlook is the fact that the one they prayed for didn't want to be healed by God.

I had a heart-breaking experience with this in 2010, when I learned that my younger brother was dying of cancer. I flew to North Carolina on short notice and spent 24 hours at his bedside praying for healing. In the midst of this, my older brother informed me that my younger brother had given up the fight to live and had already accepted death. He died a few days later. I assumed that he wanted to be healed when in fact he did not. When a person decides that they're ready to die, they are exercising their free will. God usually honors that choice. He doesn't force healing on anyone who doesn't want it.

In my adventures, I've run across many people who were reluctant about being healed. In most cases, I shared a few testimonies and asked if they would reconsider. Some allowed me to pray and some didn't. I believe we should always honor the wishes of those who don't want to be healed. There may be exceptions like when a patient is in a coma and can't express their wishes, but in general, we should refrain from praying with people who have refused prayer. The heart of the Father is such that He honors our free will, even if it leads to our own detriment and destruction. God honors free will and we should too.

CHAPTER ELEVEN

Healing 101

IT'S TIME TO DISCUSS THE practical fundamentals of healing the sick. From my own experiences and in what I've learned from those who have successfully ministered healing over decades, a common message comes forth: To operate successfully in healing it's imperative to establish a strong, active relationship with the Holy Spirit. All that we do must be led and powered by the Spirit of God.

As we minister healing to others, we're not primarily about the business of healing. We are ambassadors of heaven, facilitating new relationships with those who may not know God. If we don't know His ways, we can't share Him with the world. Establishing and maintaining our relationship with God is the first order of business. The authority to heal comes from being a disciple of Jesus. If you're not one of His disciples yet, you can become one. A disciple is a student; one who learns from a teacher. You may ask, "How do I become a disciple?" The first step is to ask Jesus to come into your heart and life. This request lets Jesus know that you want to know Him and you want Him to guide you in life – so do it sincerely.

You may ask, is it really that simple? Yes, it is. At that point, the Holy Spirit is within you even if you feel no immediate change in your body or mind. Some people experience a noticeable change while others do not. Don't be concerned if you don't notice anything different – in time you will. Start by simply understanding that Jesus said He would send the Holy Spirit to come and live in you – forever. The Holy Spirit is like a quiet voice bringing wisdom and revelation to you. His role is to "lead you into all truth" but a teacher needs a willing student. You become a disciple when you allow yourself to be taught His ways. You can learn many things about God by reading the scriptures, but the only way to know God *himself* is through the experiences you have with Him personally. I would encourage you to ask questions of the Holy Spirit and listen for His answers. This is how you develop a relationship with the living God and grow confident that He is truly guiding you. You may encounter people who will tell you that you must speak in tongues, be water baptized, or a number of other things before you truly have the Holy Spirit living in you. While all of these things are beneficial, I would caution against using them as a litmus test for proof of spiritual life. I heard the voice of God, had visions, and prophesied before I spoke in tongues or had been baptized in water.

My next bit of advice is to get rid of daily distractions and seek the face of God in solitude. Unplug your television and use the time to rest in God's presence. Sing, worship, pray, let God give you visions and dreams, do some fasting and get acquainted with Him in ways you haven't before. As your relationship with God grows so will your faith for healing. You may notice immediate answers to prayer. You may learn to pray in a language you don't understand. You might feel impressions or emotions about situations in the lives of other people that you would not otherwise know. This can be a way the Holy Spirit will lead you to pray for them.

The following advice comes from a friend, Brian Fenimore, who has been healing the sick for decades. Don't ever try to heal the sick while remaining detached from the presence of the Holy Spirit. You can heal the sick on faith or authority alone and many people have done it. When we do this, we start to believe we can heal the sick without the direct involvement of the Holy Spirit. We'll build a kingdom for ourselves, and eventually the healing dynamic will collapse. After a successful run, we may find that people aren't being healed and wonder what happened. The failure comes because we left the Holy Spirit out of the encounter. Always invite the Holy Spirit to lead the healing encounter and allow Him to do with the person what He wants done. Ministry with the Holy Spirit is a dance. He leads and we follow.

The vast majority of divine healing comes through faith. It's that simple. Children can be used in healing because they haven't been poisoned with doubt. If you have doubts about God's desire to heal the sick through you, replacing doubt with faith is critical. One way to build faith is to lay hands on anyone who will let you. At first, you may not see many people healed, but eventually you will. It depends of the level of faith you begin with. I had to overcome a lot of skepticism, but you may not and you may see miracles immediately. As I prayed with people my faith grew and the frequency of miracles increased. You should expect the same results.

When I began in healing, I found every passage in the New Testament that had to do with healing and I studied and memorized them. Then I went through the Old Testament. Reading Scripture passages about healing is a faith-building experience. Study, study, study, then rest in the Holy Spirit and let Him apply it to your spirit. One thing we all need is to have our minds renewed to the truth of God's will concerning healing, and exercises like this can help.

If you need healing, try to find someone who has had success in healing, and have them pray for you. My own healing made a profound impact on my faith for healing others. I suffered from months of shoulder pain. One day I went to a meeting where a man prayed for me. The next day I felt the pain leave and realized I was healed. Pursue your healing until you receive it.

Many people have been successful in healing before you. They all have lessons you can learn from. If you know people who operate in healing, go with them when they minister. If healing is happening at a certain place make a point to be there and witness it firsthand. Bill Johnson said, "If you want to kill giants, hang around giant-killers." There's wisdom in this principle. My daughter and wife have become proficient at healing because they've been around me when I do it and their faith has grown alongside mine.

Read books, watch videos – especially testimonies of healing and instruction. Many people who operate in healing have mp3s and podcasts you can listen to. There are many other good books that have been written about healing. I have a lot of resources on my website and part of my own training came from reviewing material I wanted to publish. Devour all you can, then rest in the Holy Spirit and let Him sort things out for you.

I receive a lot of requests for healing by e-mail. Some of the more amazing testimonies came from these long-distance requests. A number of friends do healing through an application on Facebook that utilizes the chat feature. They've amassed thousands of healing testimonies in just a few years. Thousands have been healed over Skype prayer sessions. Be open to healing over distances, particularly if praying for people in public is just too frightening for you.

Assessing a person's degree of illness or injury is something I must do as a paramedic but it's also helpful in healing. I ask the patient questions before I begin. Part of this is to establish the bridge of relationship:

1. Ask about the onset of symptoms – when and how the sickness or injury happened.

2. Ask about severity of pain on a scale from one to ten, with "1" being almost no pain and "10" being the worst pain imaginable. This is helpful in evaluating the progress of healing. If the pain was an "8" at the start and a few minutes later it's a "3", you're making progress.

3. Ask about limitations in activity or range of motion.

4. Ask how long they've had the symptoms.

5. Ask about treatment they've had. Antibiotics damage the immune system; so commanding the immune system to be healed may be in order. Radiation and chemotherapy also damage the body. You may need to command that damage to be healed. Don't be discouraged by what you hear. It's just information so that when they are healed, you'll know what they were healed of.

A good way to start is by approaching friends, family, co-workers and strangers who may need healing. When I order food at a restaurant or coffee shop they usually ask, "Is that all you need today?" Sometimes I'll reply, "That's it... unless you know someone who needs healing." I often find people with headaches or other things to heal. When I'm shopping I look for canes, casts, immobilizers, splints, wheelchairs and people hobbling along in obvious pain. These folks are usually open to healing. Introduce yourself, build some trust and ask if they would like to be healed. If they say no, bless them and keep going. Eventually you will find people who want prayer.

You'll find many different methods of healing that other people have had success with. Most of them work. Some are better than others, but none are foolproof. I saw an approach that I liked so I borrowed it then adapted it to fit my personality. It works for me but it doesn't work for everyone. Don't get hung up on following a certain method. Develop your own, as I did. In fact, you might consider using different methods at different times. Jesus used a different method nearly every time and had great success.

Among my friends who have the highest success rates in healing, there is agreement on one approach that seems to work best. It involves commanding sickness or pain to leave and commanding healing to take its place. Don't beg or plead with God to heal anyone. The most common mistake people make is begging God to heal. The second is quitting too soon. Persistence brings breakthrough. You'll have to get used to a little embarrassment. You may look a bit foolish repeatedly commanding a broken leg to be healed when there is no outward sign that it's helping. Yet the vast majority of healings I've seen came because I stood there looking like an idiot, repeatedly commanding an injury to be healed until it finally was healed.

One of the ways we can heal is by laying hands on the sick. If you're able to physically touch the sick person, it may help, but it isn't always necessary. Often times I don't touch people and they are still healed. Command sickness, disease, inflammation, pain, darkness, depression, or unclean spirits to leave. Next command organs, blood vessels, nerves, ligaments, tendons, bones, cartilage, muscles and other anatomical structures to be healed.

Yes, I said command spirits to leave. One of the things I've learned is that there are usually demons hanging around sick and injured people. I didn't say these people were possessed by spirits, but spirits are often found around sickness, disease and trauma. I've had a number of experiences where I commanded a knee or ankle to be healed and nothing happened even after five or six attempts. In some cases, I closed my eyes and God showed me a spirit that needed to be removed and in other cases I assumed a spirit was there and commanded it to leave. In almost every case, the next command brought complete healing. Remember that when the disciples could not heal the boy with seizures, Jesus removed the spirit that caused the sickness. Once the spirit was evicted, the boy was healed. If healing is going poorly consider the possibility that a spirit is present that must be removed.

Don't be discouraged if nothing happens the first time you command healing to happen. Do it again. Don't be discouraged if nothing happens the second time. Do it again. Don't give up if nothing happens the third time. Do it again. Keep commanding the affliction to leave and command the sick or injured body part to be healed. If the individual you are praying for is willing to let you continue praying, by all means – keep going. But be sensitive to their comfort level and realize that they may not have the time or desire to have you continue after a few attempts. Be courteous and consider that they may have a busy schedule. If it seems like they are uncomfortable having you continue, respect their wishes and allow them to go about their day.

When I started seeing people healed, most of it came after four or five times of commanding healing to happen. Be persistent and don't quit. If you see any change in symptoms or severity of pain after four or five times, keep going. You're making progress. If you see any change at all, you can eventually get it to go away completely.

In the Christian community where healing and miracles are common, a distinction is made between a *healing* and a *miracle*. When a person is healed through a gradual process, it is said to be a **healing**. When a condition disappears immediately, it is said to be a **miracle**. I tend not to make the distinction myself, but if you discuss healing and miracles with certain groups of people, you'll find that many of them insist on using the correct terms.

In the practice of healing, patience is worth its weight in gold. Some people will only be healed after an hour or even several hours of battling against the disease. Would your time be well spent if it took two hours to get someone healed of diabetes or blindness? Would you consider it a good use of your time if it took 15 hours to get someone healed of Lou Gehrig's disease? And would you be content to pray for a resurrection for 24 hours if that's what it took? As your faith grows, healing will take less time and the frequency of miracles should increase. As my faith has grown in the last year, most people are being healed after just one or two commands.

Commanding healing is a strong place to begin, but there are other ways to get people healed and some diseases don't respond to commands. Resist the temptation to rely on this approach exclusively, even though it works well. I see healing as a battle and like real warfare; we have a variety of weapons at our disposal. Sometimes an assault rifle is the weapon of choice. Sometimes a grenade is better and once in a while a 2,000-pound bomb is needed to get the job done. If you're having problems getting someone healed, ask God for the right weapon.

Commanding healing is like engaging in close combat with the enemy. It's effective in most cases, but it has limitations. There were times when Jesus confronted the enemy directly and times when He did not. Consider the paralytic whom He told to take up his mat and walk.

Jesus didn't command him to be healed or cast out a demon. He didn't touch him. He gave him a command to obey, which he couldn't obey unless his body was healed. His body obeyed the command and was healed, so that he could stand up. In this example, Jesus didn't even acknowledge the disease. He commanded the man to do something that required healing to happen.

Recently, the Lord has been training me to use a similar approach. In September of 2011, I received two prayer requests via Facebook for healing of tumors within a couple of days. One was a brain tumor; the other was a thyroid tumor. Both patients were about to undergo surgery within 24 hours. In both cases, when I closed my eyes to see how the Lord wanted to proceed, I saw a throne. Most of the revelation I receive about healing comes through visions.

I know from past experience that when God shows me a throne, He wants me to make a declaration as a king would. This approach doesn't involve commanding the disease to leave. I make a declaration that requires healing of the disease in order for the declaration to come to pass, just as Jesus told the paralytic to stand up. In both cases I declared that the doctors would find no tumor when they went into the operating room. I didn't command anything to leave or ask God for anything. It was a short declaration and nothing more. In order for the declaration to come to pass, the tumors would have to disappear. In both cases, I received a message the following day that when the patient was taken to the operating room, the surgeons could not find the tumors.

This is equivalent to a 2,000-pound bomb being dropped from heaven. It's quick and clean and doesn't require direct engagement of the enemy. This is just one of the many ways you can see people healed. There is one passage in the New Testament that instructs us to pray for healing:

> *Is anyone among you sick? Let him call for the elders of the church, and let them pray over him, anointing him with oil in the name of the Lord.*
> JAS. 5:14

It seems that if you are in the position of a church elder, praying for the sick may be a good approach along with anointing the sick person with oil. I have some anointing oil and I occasionally use it, but it's more for myself than for others. I'm not certain if James taught that oil was to be used symbolically or if he knew of its medicinal properties.

Many recent studies have proven that cinnamon oil has powerful anti-microbial properties and is effective against bacteria like e-coli, strep-tococcus and methicillin-resistant Staphylococcus Aureus, or MRSA.

I use a blend known as Thieves' oil. Legend has it that during the Middle Ages, thieves were able to rob the bodies of those who died from the bubonic plague without becoming sick because they used this oil to prevent sickness. Thieves' is a blend of clove, lemon, cinnamon, eucalyptus and rosemary oils. If you decide to use oils, be careful to use them as directed by the manufacturer. Some essential oils must be diluted before use.

Another way to heal is to speak words of healing over the person who is sick. I've had several dreams and visions where God instructed me in this approach. In these experiences I saw lights grow brighter when certain words were spoken. They were words such as hope, love, peace, power, spirit, life, healing, etc. Jesus said, "The words that I speak are spirit and they are life" (see Jn. 6:63). We also know that the tongue holds the power of life and death (see Prov. 18:21). We'll look at more unique methods of healing in the chapter on street healing.

Healing has limitations. It's not the ultimate answer to life's problems and it's irrelevant to healthy people. When you find yourself surrounded by a crowd of people with no healing needs and healing is your only weapon – you have nothing to give them.

Personally, I love the prophetic life. It's a gift that can be used in any situation with anyone. Who wouldn't like an encouraging word from God? Biblical dream interpretation is another great tool to have in your arsenal. Consider other gifts God might want you to use. Remember my advice on building your relationship with the Holy Spirit? If you're tuned in to what He's saying, you'll know which gift He wants to use and how He wants to use it.

And now a word of caution: If anyone claims to have figured it all out concerning healing and they tell you not to bother learning from anyone else – beware. They have an agenda that you don't want to be under. These people are out to gather a following and they probably have a desire to control others. Be open to different teachers and different approaches to healing and you'll never stop learning about the ways of God.

CHAPTER TWELVE

The Word of Knowledge

ONE OF THE TOOLS AVAILABLE to those who operate in healing is the *word of knowledge*. You may be unfamiliar with this term, so I've written this chapter to provide a simplified explanation of it. The Bible mentions the word of knowledge in Paul's letter to the church in Corinth:

> *But the manifestation of the Spirit is given to each one for the profit of all: for to one is given the word of wisdom, through the Spirit, to another the word of knowledge through the same Spirit, to another the gift of faith by the same Spirit, to another gifts of healings by the same Spirit...*
> 1 COR. 12:7-10

The word of knowledge is information given by the Holy Spirit revealing certain facts, which God is aware of, but we are not. It is information about a past or present situation that is true. The word of knowledge is considered by some to be one of three revelatory gifts, which serve as spiritual eyes and ears for the believer. The others are the *word of wisdom* and *discerning of spirits*. The word of wisdom is similar to the word of knowledge. The difference is that it gives information about what to do in a particular situation. Discerning of spirits will be discussed in the chapter on deliverance.

Just as a word is a fragment or part of a sentence, a "word" of knowledge is a fragment or a part of God's knowledge of a situation. He gives us a piece of information to aid in bringing something to pass concerning that situation. Once we receive God's revelation, it's our responsibility to ask what He wants us to do with it. If we lock it away in our hearts and don't act on it, we hinder the work He wants to do. His desire is to bless us so that we, in turn, might bless others.

Here are some of the purposes for the word of knowledge:

- To lead people to Christ
- To give direction in ministry
- To reveal sickness
- To restore the believer back to fellowship with God
- To provide encouragement

The word of knowledge can come in a number of different ways. Some people hear the voice of God speaking, while others receive a word through dreams or visions. A word of knowledge for healing often presents as a sudden pain or other sensation in our body that we don't normally have. Learning to receive a word of knowledge comes by developing sensitivity to the leading of the Holy Spirit. The revelation gifts are relational – as we develop a deeper relationship with the Holy Spirit, we grow in our awareness of how He communicates with us.

Here are some examples of the word of knowledge from Scripture:

Jesus frequently received words of knowledge. He told two of His disciples to go into a village and get a donkey that no man had ever ridden before, telling them where to find the donkey (see Lk. 19:30, 31). While talking with the woman at the well of Samaria, He said to her, "Go, call your husband, and come here." The woman answered and said, "I have no husband." Jesus said to her, "You have well said, 'I have no husband,' for you have had five husbands, and the one whom you now have is not your husband..." The woman said to Him, "Sir, I perceive that You are a prophet" (see Jn. 4:16-19). In this case, the word of knowledge led to the revelation of who Jesus was.

Peter received a word of knowledge in a vision, when God revealed that the gospel was for Gentiles as well as Jews. As he pondered the first bit of information, the first Gentiles arrived at his front door. God told him that three men were looking for him and that he should meet with them, doubting nothing (see Acts 10:9-20).

Ananias received a word of knowledge in a vision concerning a new believer named Saul of Tarsus:

> *And there was a certain disciple at Damascus named Ananias... so the Lord said to him, "Arise and go to the street called Straight, and inquire at the house of Judas for one called Saul of Tarsus, for behold, he is praying. And in a vision he has seen a man named Ananias coming in and putting his hand on him, so that he might receive his sight."*
> ACTS 9:10-12

There are words of knowledge recorded in both Old and New Testaments. Through a word of knowledge, Samuel told Saul that the donkeys that were lost had been found (see 1 Sam. 9:19-20). When the king of Syria made war against Israel, the Lord spoke to Elisha through a word of knowledge to reveal the enemy's plan (see 2 Kgs. 6:9-12).

The word of knowledge can encourage us. Jezebel was out to kill Elijah. Out of fear, he ran and sat under a juniper tree and begged God to let him die, thinking he was the only prophet left. But God encouraged Elijah by telling him; "I have 7,000 in Jerusalem who have not bowed their knee to Baal" (see 1 Kgs. 19:18).

A word of knowledge can alert us to a condition that God would like us to address. But a word of knowledge isn't a guarantee that the person will be healed. Until we take action, it's only information. If we don't enforce God's will concerning the word given, nothing will change.

A word of knowledge might be given by the Holy Spirit to let some-one with a certain condition know that they can be healed. This is sometimes the case when a person doubts the will of God about their healing. But it can also be used to make us aware that someone we're about to meet has a condition we should pray for.

A word of knowledge may be given to encourage us to pray for a condi-tion we wouldn't normally have faith to heal. One of the first words of knowledge I received was for a man with Lou Gehrig's disease. At this point in my life I had no faith that I'd ever see this condition healed. When I gave the word to him and his wife, it boosted their hope.

I received a word of knowledge in a dream about healing people with birth defects. When I returned to work after two days off duty, my first patient was a girl with Down syndrome, which I wouldn't normally have much faith for. But because of the dream, I prayed with confidence when we transported her.

While at an airport, I received a word of knowledge while waiting in line at a coffee stand. I suddenly felt the presence of God come upon me. I instinctively closed my eyes. The Lord showed me an image in my mind of a middle-aged woman and the word "migraine." I looked around the terminal for her, but I didn't see anyone who resembled her. During the flight, while reading the book *Power Healing* by John Wimber, I decided to take a break and closed the book. I looked up and saw the woman God showed me in the vision. She was waiting in line to use the restroom. I walked over and asked if she had migraine headaches. She said she did and she allowed me to pray with her.

Words of knowledge can be given to us in unusual ways. God sometimes focuses our attention on a particular person – making them stand out in a crowd. Some of us receive words of knowledge which manifest as a sudden sensation of pain, warmth or tingling. This is often a word of knowledge for healing that part of the body for someone nearby.

Many people receive words of knowledge and don't know it. One day I developed a sharp pain in the back of my hand while walking through a grocery store on duty. I had done nothing to injure my hand. I wasn't certain, but I thought perhaps it was a word of knowledge. So I began asking people around me if they had pain in their hand, but no one did. I finally told my EMT partner about it. He told me that he fell out of a tree a week earlier and had been having pain in the same spot in his hand all week. I prayed for his hand and it was healed. When you feel a sudden pain you can't explain, consider the possibility that the Holy Spirit is giving you a word of knowledge for someone.

One of the more unusual words of knowledge I ever received was about a problem I had while replacing the timing belt on my car. After putting everything back together, the car wouldn't start. I checked the service manual and looked at the timing marks again, but I couldn't find the problem. I closed my eyes and asked God what the problem was. In a vision, I saw the camshaft gear and noticed that it had two timing marks. I was aware of only one. The mark I used was the wrong one. After locating the other timing mark and making the correction, the car ran perfectly.

If you'd like to receive words of knowledge, ask God to reveal things to you and spend time getting to know His ways. The revelation gifts are relational and time is the commodity of relationships. I spent an entire winter (our slow season) lying on the bench in the back of the ambulance. I spent hours and days and weeks just lying there quietly with my eyes closed. Whenever I had my eyes closed, God revealed things to me in visions.

The images would remain in view until I guessed what they meant. Over time I became more accurate in interpreting them and the right interpretation didn't take as many guesses. The Holy Spirit was training me. As the months passed, the nature of the visions changed. They began as 2-dimensional, flat images, then after a while they became 3-dimensional images. Then they began to move and appeared more like videos. Eventually I began seeing transparent beings and multiple scenes that overlapped.

Whether we receive words of knowledge through impressions, visions, dreams, pain in our body or the still small voice of the Holy Spirit, it takes time to hone and develop the gift. The Holy Spirit is the giver of the gift, so ask Him for revelation, be sensitive to His leading and obey when He leads.

CHAPTER THIRTEEN

Healing: A Tool for Evangelism and a Gift

WHEN I SHARE MY STORIES about healing, Christians sometimes ask, "Did you share the gospel with them?"

This question supposes that healing is to be used in conjunction with preaching the gospel. While it's true that healing provides a great benefit to the work of evangelism, it isn't the only purpose God has for it. Healing can also keep believers healthy. The combination of preaching the gospel and healing miracles is perhaps the most convincing way to display the nature of God and His kingdom. The apostle Paul wrote,

> *And my speech and my preaching were not with persuasive words of human wisdom, but in demonstration of the Spirit and of power, that your faith should not be in the wisdom of men but in the power of God.*
>
> 1 COR. 2:4-5

I've heard many testimonies from African missionaries where people have been healed of incurable diseases, set free of demonic oppression, raised from the dead, and where thousands were brought into a relationship with Jesus as a result of these powerful works. Healing and other displays of God's power should always confirm the message of the gospel. But evangelism is only one of the purposes God has for healing.

Healing is also a gift to the Church, from God. As such, its intended purpose is to maintain the overall health of the body of Christ. Healing as a gift to the Church has no connection to the gospel being preached, because the Church doesn't need to evangelize itself.

We looked at this passage in the previous chapter, but let's look at it once more:

> *But the manifestation of the Spirit is given to each one for the profit of all: for to one is given the word of wisdom, through the Spirit, to another the word of knowledge through the same Spirit, to another the gift of faith by the same Spirit, to another gifts of healings by the same Spirit...*
> 1 COR. 12:7-9

Just as with the other gifts of the Holy Spirit, the gifts of healings (yes, they are plural) are given to edify and strengthen the Church. What is implied here is important; if healing is a gift from God, then it must be His desire for the Church to be healthy. Let me say that in another way: It is not God's will for the Church to be sick. The gifts of healings are God's way of keeping the Church healthy and the gifts work, as long as we operate in them.

Every believer has been given authority over sickness. Some of us exercise it more than others. The authority to heal in connection with preaching the gospel is resident and available at all times to every believer. But the *gifts* function differently. The gifts are not used for evangelism. They are a separate work God does for the purpose of keeping the church healthy. They operate under the discretion of the Holy Spirit. At times, He may have us operate in the gifts of healings, at other times in discerning of spirits, and other times we might prophesy. The gifts of the Holy Spirit are subject to the mind of God at any given time.

On occasion, I've been used in healing for the purpose of evangelism, but more often I function in the *gifts* of healings for strengthening the Church body. I also tend to operate in the gifts of prophecy and discerning of spirits. God tends to use me more in these gifts, but not everyone is called in the same way. If you aren't certain what God's calling is for you, I'd encourage you to ask Him.

My friend Craig Adams had this to say about healing as a gift:

> As a gift for the edification and strengthening of the Body of Christ, the value of the gifts of healing goes far beyond the physical health of its members. When healing gifts are exercised, the faith of both the one healed and the one healing is built up and becomes stronger. Faith not only in God, but faith in one's ability to do the works Jesus did, as He said we would.

> Many who might otherwise move powerfully in the gifts of the Spirit are not lacking faith in God to want to do them, but in themselves and their own ability to be instrumental in ministering the gifts. I believe that it was due to a similar lack of faith in themselves that Jesus rebuked the disciples when He calmed the storm on the lake after the multiplication of loaves and fishes. It says they 'considered not the loaves and fishes'. Rabbi Yeshua merely spoke the blessing over the food and told them what to do. It was by their hand that a boy's lunch was distributed to feed thousands with basketsful left over.

> Healing is not only for evangelism, but also for the building up of the physical and spiritual health of believers.

I like the fact that God gives us the power to heal merely for the benefits that healing itself provides. There's no reason to feel pressured to preach the gospel every time someone is healed. If the one you're praying with doesn't know Jesus, by all means lead them to Him. But if evangelism isn't your strong suit, you can still function powerfully in healing. You may want to partner with people who are strong in evangelism, so that when it's needed, the opportunity isn't wasted.

CHAPTER FOURTEEN

Street Healing

JESUS WAS THE ORIGINAL STREET healer. He traveled the streets of Israel on foot, staying wherever He found lodging. During His travels He told people the secrets of their hearts, healed all who were sick and demon-possessed, raised the dead and shared the mysteries of the kingdom of God. This was His lifestyle and it could be yours.

After modeling this lifestyle, Jesus chose twelve disciples and gave them their commission. He gave them power, authority and some guidelines (see Matt 10:5-14). He told them to:

- Visit the cities of Israel
- Inquire who was worthy
- Speak peace to the homes that received them
- Preach on the kingdom of God
- Deal with sickness and demonic oppression

Things went well on their first assignment. So well, that a short time later He sent out seventy disciples to do the same things, with a few changes to the plan (see Lk. 10:1-10).

This was the model Jesus established for His Church. How strange it is to look at the Church today and marvel that we've strayed so far from the only example He ever gave us. One of the saddest truths about Christendom is the fact that in most cities there are more than a dozen churches, but not one person with the faith to heal cancer.

An important aspect of street healing is geographic; being in the right place is critical. The disciples were given specific instructions where to minister and where not to. Jesus told them not to go to Samaria (see Mt. 10:5). In the book of Acts we read that the disciples tried to go to several places that the Holy Spirit didn't want them to visit:

> *Now when they had gone through Phrygia and the region of Galatia, they were forbidden by the Holy Spirit to preach the word in Asia. After they had come to Mysia, they tried to go into Bithynia, but the Spirit did not permit them. So passing by Mysia, they came down to Troas.*
> ACTS 16:6-8

Jesus set the stage for the disciples' ministry to bear fruit. We don't know why the Holy Spirit opposed their ministry to Asia and Bithynia. Perhaps these regions weren't prepared yet, while other regions were.

If you're considering healing the sick in your hometown there are a few things you might consider. Jesus faced opposition when He attempted to heal the sick in his hometown. Many of us have experienced the disappointment of trying to minister to our families. Those who know our faults and failures from childhood may doubt that God could use us. I'm not saying you can't be used by God in your hometown, but if you meet resistance and failure, consider asking God if there is another location where He could use you. It may be a good idea to periodically ask Him for information on where you can be used most effectively.

Another aspect of street healing is relational; Jesus instructed His disciples to find people who were worthy. He not only told them there were certain places to go, but that there were certain people who would receive them and others who would not. How many of us have been frustrated by an experience where we poured all we had into a group of people and it seemed all our labor was for nothing? God has certain people in mind whose hearts have been prepared for our message. They're ready for us to reveal God's love and grace to them, but we must find out who and where they are.

Jesus knew He could visit the pool of Bethesda and find someone who was lame or crippled, because they often gathered there, waiting for an angel to stir the waters. It became a regular hang-out for the sick and infirmed. Anyone wanting to be used by God to heal the sick could go there.

There are several places street healers visit because they know they'll find people there who need healing. One is the local hospital – especially the emergency department. Many emergency departments have long waiting times before patients can be seen by a doctor. Hospitals offer no cure for most chronic conditions like fibromyalgia, migraine headaches and back pain. All they have to offer is temporary relief in the form of a prescription. Emergency Departments have proven to be an excellent location for healing. Just be mindful that you obey hospital policies and be respectful. If you don't create too much disruption, you're less likely to be asked to leave.

I became aware of the fact that there is a library for the blind in downtown Phoenix. They lend Braille and audio books to the visually impaired. Imagine how easy it would be to sit outside a library like this each day for a few hours asking patrons if they would like to have their eyesight restored.

Another location frequented by street healers is Walmart. Jose Coelho calls it a "Christian's Disneyland," because so many healing testimonies have come out of Walmart stores in recent years. Why Walmart? Many of their customers have conditions that need healing. In comparison to other retail stores, Walmart has a much higher rate of shoppers using wheelchairs, canes, crutches, immobilizers and hearing aids. I've seen a number of people healed at Walmart including the first person I ever saw healed of carpal tunnel syndrome.

Revelation and Observation

There are two ways we can find people who need healing. The first is the most obvious; as you travel during your day, look around and see if you notice anyone wearing a cast, a splint, an immobilizer, wearing dark sunglasses inside (possible blindness), hearing aids, walking with a cane or sitting in a wheelchair. I often approach people who walk unevenly, which may be due to arthritis or some other disease. Simple observation will reveal dozens of people you could provide healing to. Now consider all the people you'll meet in a week who talk openly about migraine headaches, back pain, fibromyalgia, cancer treatments and other medical conditions. If you add them to the list, the number would be rather large.

On several occasions, I've awakened from a dream where I was praying with someone. Later in the day, I found the person I met in the dream and prayed with them. We already discussed words of knowledge, which are ways that God can lead you to people who need to be healed. The process is to receive the revelation, interpret it, and then find the person God wants to heal.

God will heal people, regardless of how you find them. Revelation through words of knowledge is a great way to locate people with conditions that aren't obvious. If you're sensitive to the leading of the Holy Spirit, you'll find it easy to hear, see or "just know" what God wants to do for them.

But remember, receiving a word of knowledge for someone may not be a guarantee they'll be healed. The person may not even allow you to pray for them. I was once given an accurate word of knowledge for a woman who was in line at Starbuck's. The Holy Spirit showed me she had trouble with migraines, but when I approached her, she wouldn't let me pray for her. If you're wondering why God would give someone a word of knowledge, knowing it wouldn't be received, consider that it might have planted a seed in her heart. Maybe the woman went home that night and had a dream about a stranger who was concerned about her headaches – and the stranger in the dream happened to look just like Jesus. Never underestimate the craftiness of God. He can bring value out of a situation that seems puzzling to us on the surface.

Two by Two

Jesus sent out the seventy disciples in groups of two (see Lk. 10:1). Have you ever wondered why? I didn't, until I began this journey into healing and not long afterward, it became obvious. Success and humility don't always walk hand in hand, though they do make a handsome couple. One of the problems we encounter in healing is the tendency for pride to sneak into our lives when miracles happen. If there are two pairs of hands resting on someone when they're healed of cancer, who gets the credit? One reason for doing ministry in tandem is to prevent swollen egos. The honor and glory belongs to God. Partnering with others can prevent opportunities for pride to take root.

Another reason is that we all struggle at times with obedience or consistency. Having a partner can minimize the effect of those days when your faith is weak or you are in rebellion. Your partner should be praying for you and you should be praying for them. Healing is warfare, but it's warfare done from a place of rest. Our victory comes from what Jesus has already done; all we do is inform the world that the victory has been won. Once you begin to heal the sick, the enemy is likely to take notice and bring some resistance your way. Don't be afraid; it's only a fear campaign to get you to quit. Rest in the knowledge that you are more than a conqueror (see Rom. 8:37).

I have a few trusted friends who are gifted in discernment. Our time together is always beneficial. They're attentive to the details of my spiritual life. They usually detect the "gunk" the enemy has tried to hang on me since the last time we met. They clean up my armor and I clean up theirs. When you're in battle, you're going to take a few fiery darts from the enemy. Don't go into battle alone. Having a partner can be a great benefit.

My primary partner for ministry is my wife. There are a lot of good reasons why you might consider involving your spouse. The enemy would like to ruin as many of us as possible. How many big ministries have crashed and burned after a scandalous affair? I don't want to give the enemy an opportunity to destroy me or my marriage, so whenever possible, my wife and I minister together. She has the password to my e-mail account and all my social networking profiles. When I'm on

Facebook, she's usually a few feet away on her computer – not because she doesn't trust me, but because she's interested in what I do and she wants to protect me from potential dangers.

Some people have had great success in healing by going on "treasure hunts." A "treasure hunt" is when a group of people gather and spend a few minutes asking God for revelation about who He wants to touch. God gives clues, like names, articles of clothing, illnesses, or images of their surroundings. They write down the clues then go out in search of the people based on the clues.

This is a great way to practice hearing from God. If you're afraid to go out in public by yourself, doing it in a group may be a safer approach. Treasure hunts partner more experienced healers with beginners and allow beginners a chance to see God at work. They're also a biblical model of ministry since Jesus sent His disciples into the community two by two. Finally, treasure hunts, because they require God to lead you to certain people, are likely to be more effective than approaching people at random.

I watched a video testimony from a woman who went on her first treasure hunt with a group of friends. The clues led them to a woman in a wheelchair at a bus stop who had multiple sclerosis. They asked the woman in the wheelchair if they could pray with her and she agreed. After prayer, she was healed. She got up from the wheelchair, thanked them and got on a bus, leaving the wheelchair behind.

In practice, we can lay hands on people for healing or stand a few feet away. We can command healing silently or out loud and we'll probably see the same results. The sick were healed by the anointing that was on the Apostle Paul's handkerchiefs and aprons. I love Pete Cabrera's illustration of this principle, when he commanded a plastic spoon to heal the sick and two people were healed by holding onto the spoon. Lisa Fitzgerald-Adams released healing bubbles on a young man with an ankle injury from skateboarding. Tom Fischer once healed someone by having them hold onto a rock that he prayed over. Jason Chin re-created the "shadow of Peter" effect by walking near a woman who was healed of a shoulder injury as his shadow passed over her. Had I had not seen the videos, I wouldn't have believed these stories. I've heard many testimonies of healing that came by speaking the word of God over the sick. There is no reason why we should limit healing to a certain method. Be creative and let God amaze you.

As your familiarity with the ways of God grows, you'll be able to see things that can only be seen with your spiritual eyes. I have friends who have developed the ability to see things in the spirit with amazing accuracy. They see "devices" that are impaled into people, like spears, swords or metal bars. It's common to see serpents coiled around people or metal bands around parts of their body. In most cases, these devices require removal. The act of removing an impaled object, cutting a metal band or removing a serpent may bring immediate healing. These things are done by faith, believing that what you see in the spirit is real and its effect will cease if the object is removed. After the device is dealt with, there may be wounds (in the spirit) that require prayer for healing. Pay attention to the wounds you're shown and keep praying until they either disappear or the person tells you they believe the healing process has been completed.

The streets and shops you visit are full of people who desperately need to know that God cares about them. All around you, crippled people struggle to cope. The blind are robbed of experiencing the abundant life Jesus died to give them. You are the one who can release the power that changes those circumstances. Street healing is easy; it just takes a little compassion, a little boldness, some faith, and a desire to see God's love in action. This is the model Jesus gave us. And if a skeptic like me can be used to heal the sick, so can you.

CHAPTER FIFTEEN

Healing in the Workplace

THE FIRST TEN VERSES OF Luke chapter 5 describe what happened to Peter when he allowed his workplace to be a platform for the ministry of Jesus. After the Lord taught from Peter's boat, He asked him to go into deeper water and let down his nets. After telling Jesus he'd been fishing all night without catching anything he reluctantly obeyed. He was astounded when the catch was so great it began to sink the boat, requiring help from others to bring it in. God blessed Peter, James and John with an immediate increase in their business when they allowed their occupation to be used by Him. Just as He did with the fishermen, God wants to bless us when we're willing to be used by Him where we work.

One day, while working on the ambulance, my regular partner took the day off. I worked with someone I didn't know very well. Megan and I were having a slow day. We were five hours into the shift and hadn't

129

run a call. To help the time pass, we talked about different things that interested us, including one of my favorite subjects – dreams.

I shared a few dreams I'd had about healing, which led to a discussion of healing itself. I shared a few healing stories, which prompted her to tell me about the car accident she was in a few years ago that left her with chronic pain between her shoulder blades. We talked and I gained her trust. So when I asked if she wanted to be healed she was comfortable having me pray with her. I explained the process then put my hand on her back and commanded it to be healed and it was.

Many of us would like to introduce our co-workers to Jesus, but our attempts often fail. Sometimes we fail because we don't know them well enough for them to receive our testimony. Sometimes our testimony lacks relevance to their needs. To someone with a medical condition that is no better after being treated by doctors, a Jesus who can heal them is extremely relevant.

In the short time I've been healing people at work, I've been amazed at the number of co-workers wanting to ask me how it works. I never wonder any more how I'll tell a co-worker about Jesus. As people are healed and word gets around, they come to me wanting to know more. I suspect that might be why Jesus trained His disciples in healing.

The degree to which you'll minister to anyone is dependent on the relationship you have with them. Asking a stranger if they want to be healed isn't something most people do. They're bound to wonder what's in it for you. Expect to have your motives questioned. Think about why you want to heal strangers so when they ask, you'll have an answer. With a stranger, it's helpful to engage in safe conversation, allowing them a few minutes to evaluate your motives. If the one who needs healing is someone you know – the relationship may already be strong enough for prayer.

As we minister in the workplace, we should remember a few things; Jesus healed all who came to Him, but many chose not to come. As badly as we may want others to receive God's healing touch, we must always ask permission and respect the wishes of those who say no. If we show honor and respect, it will be shown to us, even from those who disagree with us. *"When a man's ways please the Lord, He makes even his enemies to be at peace with him"* (see Prov. 16:7).

Another thing to keep in mind is that employers hire us to work and they have a right to expect us to be productive. We should want to make our employer successful. If we spend too much time engaged in ministry at work and it interferes with productivity or proficiency, they may need to take corrective action. We should treat customers and co-workers well and be diligent in our duties. When we're good employees, we fulfill the command to "do all things as unto the Lord."

A generation ago, it was common for people to talk about their faith in the workplace. Today, separatists and secularists are trying hard to ban public discussions of faith. Workplace discussions about God are becoming a risky proposition. In some parts of the world discussing Jesus puts you at risk for harassment, punishment or termination. Many people believe we have no right to engage in religious discussions while on the job. Make no mistake; if you hope to be an outspoken disciple of Jesus, there will always be a cost to consider.

At the outset, I had some concerns that God would not heal the people I prayed with and that I would look foolish. Concerns about how we're perceived by others are sometimes rooted in pride. In my case, I had to choose obedience over what others thought about me. Humility allows us to take risks at the expense of our ego. My fears were short-lived. I did go through a season of praying with people who weren't healed, but not because God didn't want them healed. It was because I didn't know what I was doing. After changing my approach and commanding healing instead of begging God to do it, the number of people who were healed increased dramatically. I never experienced the things I'd feared. I suppose the enemy may have been trying to discourage me. He'll probably try it with you, so be brave if God asks you to heal in your workplace.

Rules regarding discussions of faith vary depending on your occupation and where you work. Check with your employer and regulatory agencies to learn what restrictions apply to you. The medical industry allows some people to discuss faith openly with patients. If you're on the pastoral staff you're allowed a lot of freedom. These positions enjoy a privileged status the rest of us don't have. There seems to be a trend toward more restriction on workplace discussions of faith. This trend needs to be challenged and the responsibility falls on us. If you work in a place where you aren't free to talk about God, it's your responsibility to engage in discussions with management to have the rules changed.

If our attempts to bring Jesus into the workplace cause customers to go elsewhere or co-workers to file complaints, perhaps we should re-think our strategy. After years of "witnessing" to people on the job, and having no fruit come from it, I began to offer healing prayer instead. In all the time I've used this approach, I haven't had a complaint from anyone. Many people have been healed, and those who were not healed were grateful that I offered to pray with them.

There are many ways in which healing can be brought to the workplace. I keep my eyes open for anyone walking in a way that shows they're in pain or suggests they are disabled. I tune in to certain conversations and tune others out, listening for medical words. After a bit of practice you'll become more perceptive to the needs of others. It's surprising how many people discuss their health problems in public. When someone discusses a surgery, a chronic painful condition or even something like insomnia, there's a need for healing standing in front of you. All you need to do is politely ask about the condition, maybe share a testimony of healing and ask if they'll let you pray with them.

After a few people are healed, your co-workers will begin to talk. As word gets around, you'll find more opportunities. As more people are healed, your faith will grow and you'll probably see more miracles. One day you'll realize that asking a stranger if they want prayer is no longer considered "risky behavior" but a normal activity.

The disciples of Jesus became habitual healers. They kept routines and visited certain places often. And wherever they went, the sick were healed and the dead were raised. They became so well known for healing, and their routines so regular that people laid the sick in their path, knowing that sickness and disease would leave. There's nothing keeping you from developing this same kind of reputation for healing. It's a matter of how much compassion you have and how closely you want to follow in the steps of Jesus.

CHAPTER SIXTEEN

Healing in Health Care

I'VE BEEN FORTUNATE TO HAVE the opportunity to see many people healed in the setting of emergency medicine. I think healing and medicine make a wonderful partnership, though not everyone agrees. There are many issues that need to be considered if you want to use divine healing in your medical practice. In this chapter, we'll discuss the most common problems and look at some solutions.

Before I began operating in divine healing, one of the things that bothered me about claims of healing miracles, was the apparent lack of credible testimonies from medical experts. The few stories I'd heard were reported in such a way that made their verification impossible. Symptoms were poorly described, no diagnosis or mention of medical treatments was given and little was provided in the way of diagnostic testing afterward to verify the claims of healing. I found these stories hard to take seriously.

Since then I've learned that a lot of clinical research has been done on healing prayer and much of it suggests that the power of prayer can be observed and predicted through clinical trials.

In 1988, Randolph Byrd shocked the world with the results of a study he had conducted five years earlier on the effects of prayer on cardiac patients. Byrd studied 393 patients admitted to a coronary care unit in a San Francisco hospital. The patients were "statistically inseparable," meaning their conditions and symptoms were all similar.

Patients were randomly assigned to one of two groups – those who received intercessory prayer and those who didn't. Neither the doctor nor the patients knew who was in which group. Byrd gave the first name, diagnosis and condition of patients in the prayer group to different groups of three or four active Christians from several denominations. These groups prayed for their patient daily throughout the patient's stay, away from the hospital, without meeting the patient. They prayed for a timely, easy recovery and one free from complications.

When the study concluded, Byrd found that there was indeed a significant difference in the quality of recovery among patients who received prayer: The prayer group fared better on average than their fellow patients who did not receive prayer. Almost 85 % of the prayer group scored "good" on the rating system used by hospitals to rate a patient's response to treatment. They were less likely to have a heart attack, need antibiotics or require interventions like ventilation or intubation. By contrast, only 73.1% of members of the control group scored "good."

Research on prayer has nearly doubled in the past ten years, says David Larson, MD, MSPH, president of the National Institute for Healthcare Research, a private nonprofit agency. Even the National Institutes of Health (NIH), which refused to review a study with the word "prayer" in it four years ago, is now funding one prayer study through its Frontier Medicine Initiative.

A survey conducted in the year 2000 evaluated scores of studies on the power of prayer and other types of distant healing. The researchers found 23 studies that featured high-quality methodologies (the steps used in experiments to measure results and control for external influences).

Of these studies, 57% found significant results supporting distant prayer's positive impact on health.

Larry Dossey, M.D. wrote a book titled *Healing Words* in which he discusses many clinical trials that have been done on healing, concluding that supernatural healing is indeed a clinically observable phenomenon.

Western medicine has experienced some worrisome trends recently. Antibiotic drug therapy is a major component of conventional medicine. Some of the most common bacteria have adapted to the drugs used to combat them. There is now a very serious problem with drug-resistant strains of bacteria. There are a number of bacteria for which there is no known treatment. These microbes have become resistant to all antibiotics. More are becoming drug-resistant every year. At some point in the future the medical community will be able to offer little in the way of treatment for what were once easily treated conditions.

Dr. Barbara Starfield of the Johns Hopkins School of Hygiene and Public Health describes how the world's most expensive health care system contributes to poor health and even death. In 2000, a large study was done that revealed a startling fact; being treated in our medical system is the third leading cause of death in America.[1] An estimated 250,000 people die every year as a result of iatrogenic causes (those related to medical treatment). Only heart disease and cancer kill more people. Among the combined causes of iatrogenic death, drug complications (not related to dosing) were the leading killer.

- 106,000 from negative effects of drugs
- 80,000 from infections in hospitals
- 20,000 from other errors in hospitals
- 12,000 from unnecessary surgery
- 7,000 from medication errors in hospitals

Today, we are unable to obtain some of the drugs commonly used for treating critically ill patients. Due to nation-wide shortages, there is a routine back order on many drugs, including some that are the staples of treating cardiac arrest. This isn't a new problem; shortages have

---

1. Journal of the American Medical Association Volume 284 July 26, 2000

plagued health care for the last five years. At the time of this writing, several EMS systems have opted to use expired drugs, feeling that this option is better than having no drugs at all. Medical practitioners are stuck in an uncomfortable position. Our trusted drugs are either not doing their job or they're harder to obtain. If the drugs we depend on are no longer readily available – how do we proceed with our treatment?

Advances in traditional medicine will continue, but they will eventually plateau. Research in the field of divine healing is just getting started. Duke University, John Hopkins and other medical centers are building programs to study and harness the full potential of spiritual healing. The landscape of health care is rapidly changing. Here is a glimpse of what it may look like in the future:

In February of 2011, I had a dream in which I watched a new hospital being built. I walked to the construction site every day to check on the progress, taking a different route each day, trying to find the shortest one.

One day I arrived as the building was nearing completion. I walked to the street corner and began walking up a steep sidewalk next to the building. There was a handrail, so I used it to climb the long, steep slope. I met a man coming down the sidewalk. He was tall and austere in appearance. He was one of the hospital staff. As we met, he glared at me and kept walking.

There was one more element in the dream; in the beginning of the dream, I watched hospital employees standing around a bed, speaking curses that were damaging a patient. They seemed to be unaware of what they were doing. At the end of the dream, when the hospital was completed, the same group of people stood in the same room and prayed for a patient, who was healed by their prayers.

Let's do some interpretation:

I believe the new hospital represents a new model of health care that God is "building." My trips to the construction site reveal my involvement (and probably the involvement of people like me) in "seeing" the new model of health care as it is built. The fact that I took a different way each day, trying to find the shortest route would suggest there are longer and shorter paths to seeing the project completed. Our influence is intended to get it done in the most expedient and efficient way possible. The steep sidewalk is a reminder that we have an "uphill battle" in helping the medical community see the value of divine healing. The austere man is a representative of the existing medical paradigm. While they may be left "speechless" by what they witness happening, they may not react favorably. Finally, the group of people who cursed the patient in the beginning and prayed for their healing in the end, could reveal a present problem and the solution to it.

The problem is that many health care workers speak words to their patients that rob them of hope and cause them to agree with sickness and death. We have enormous power in our words and people hold our views in high esteem. When we tell a patient there is no hope for survival, they tend to believe it. They give up hope, even ruling out the miraculous. If we neglect to tell patients that God wants to heal them, we've concealed from them what is perhaps the most important fact of all.

The solution is to speak frankly about their chances of survival from a medical standpoint. If medicine has nothing to offer, tell them so. And point them to the fact that God isn't limited in the ways that we are. We need to give them hope that a miracle is always *possible*, even if we don't believe it's *likely*. That option should never be taken from them. If we truly want the best outcomes for our patients, I think that includes praying for them to be healed.

Divine healing and medicine may seem like strange partners. Divine healing is a matter of faith. Medicine is mostly a matter of science. Our culture has at times identified these two as being in conflict with one another. But the truth is, divine healing is an excellent complement to the practice of medicine. There are many conditions for which medicine has little to offer. The power of divine healing has virtually no limitations. While patients have a high degree of trust in the medical community, most patients also believe in a higher power.

When God challenged me to begin praying for my patients, I had some anxiety over it. I wasn't afraid to pray silently for patients. That doesn't take a lot of faith. It was the idea of asking a stranger if they wanted me to pray with them that terrified me. I was also afraid someone would complain to my manager.

In the last few years I've prayed in public for several thousand people. About half of these were on the job and half were at stores and other public places. I have prayed for very few people in church settings. That's right – I pray for many more people outside of church than inside. Of all the patients I've asked, I can only remember a few who declined. Keep in mind that I did all this in the pacific-northwest where church attendance is the lowest in the US. My observation is this: if you're afraid that your patients don't want you praying with them – you're probably wrong. More people are willing to receive prayer than you might think. This is especially true when a patient believes they are seriously ill or on the verge of death.

When I began asking patients about prayer, I wasn't prepared for what I would find. I couldn't believe how many people not only welcomed prayer, but were deeply touched when I asked. Many cried tears of joy simply because a stranger asked if he could pray with them. This might be due to the fact that western culture views prayer as very personal. When we take a personal experience and share it publicly, it tends to bring a lot of emotion with it. I have even been surprised at how many agnostics, atheists, and people of other faiths who wanted me to pray with them. The ones who saw no immediate healing were grateful. The ones who were healed were ecstatic.

Operating as a divine healer in health care is rewarding but it does come with challenges. I have met a few people who objected to a paramedic praying with his patients on duty. I had a discussion with a doctor who was offended when she learned that I talked to my patients about God. In her mind my actions were unethical. She believes patients are vulnerable, seeing medical workers as experts. Her fear was that I would abuse my "expert" status and push a vulnerable patient into accepting a religious point of view, without having time to fully consider it. Sadly, Christians have developed a reputation for using high-pressure tactics to convert people to Christianity. While some people may operate this way, it can be a subtle form of manipulation. Is there a reason why discussions can't occur that allow us to share ideas about faith and God without crossing the lines of sound ethical practice?

When I ask a patient if I can pray with them, I have only two things in mind. One is to get them healed; the other is to introduce them to God in a way that is personal and memorable. I simply invite God to touch them in a way that will allow them to know He is real. And they are fully aware that's what I'm doing. I allow them to hear me as I ask God to touch them. I don't preach to them and I'm not in the habit of asking them to believe in Jesus as their savior.

If your motive for praying with a patient is to convert them to your religious belief, people have a right to question your motives. If on the other hand, your desire is to see your patients healed, your motives will be seen as less selfish and more consistent with the goals of sound patient care.

If medicine is about delivering the highest level of care and the best customer service possible, then divine healing should be a part of what we do, at least for those interested in the realm of faith. Yes, there are cultural obstacles to overcome. But at the time of this writing, I am aware of no legal restrictions (in the US) that prevent us from pursuing this avenue of care. Please consult a legal expert in your area to determine if there are restrictions where you live.

Weighing the Risk

Can we expect a few complaints? I suppose we should. Not long after I began praying with my patients I was called into my manager's office. A nurse in one of the emergency departments saw me praying with a patient and filed a complaint with her manager. Her manager and mine had a talk about it. I found it a bit ironic that this happened at of all places, a Catholic hospital. I work for one of the largest private ambulance services in the country. In asking his supervisors what he should do about the complaint, my manager discovered some surprising news. None of the managers in our company could recall ever dealing with an employee caught praying with a patient.

In our meeting, I explained that God asked me to pray for the people I transport. I told my manager I always ask permission before praying and I always respect the wishes of those who say no. He said our company had no policy regarding prayer on the job and there were no plans to change that. My manager's position was very reasonable. His only concern was that I avoid behavior that might generate complaints from our customers. He respected my convictions about prayer. He said I would be allowed to continue praying for patients under two conditions; first, I had to ask permission and second, I agreed to confine it to the back of the ambulance. In practice, the second one is more difficult to do as the following story happened a few weeks later:

I transported a patient from one hospital to another for a risky procedure. When a doctor inserted a tube in the patient's chest, he accidentally punctured her lung and the tube became embedded in the lung tissue. She developed a pneumothorax and rapidly declined. She was sedated, intubated and placed on a ventilator. We transferred her to a trauma hospital for emergency surgery.

During the transfer between hospitals I asked if she wanted me to pray with her and she nodded in agreement. We prayed in the ambulance. But when we were on the elevator inside the hospital, with two fire-fighters and two nurses looking on, she suddenly grabbed my hands and made a motion as if we were praying. I asked if she wanted to pray and she frantically nodded her head. So I had to pray with her in front of them. I told my manager about it. He smiled and told me not to worry about it.

Most fire departments and hospitals have some type of chaplain service for their customers, including hospitals with no religious affiliation. Becoming a part of the chaplain's service may open doors for you to pray with patients and family members, perhaps even staff. The fact that we have these services demonstrates a belief that the spiritual needs of our patients are real and that meeting those needs is a legitimate part of the service we provide.

I would like to know how an organization that advocates spiritual care in one sense, could reprimand an employee for providing it in the normal duties of their job, merely because they don't have the title of "chaplain." There is no reason why we should receive disciplinary action because we pray for patients who request it. And there is no reason to believe that any special training or certification is needed to provide spiritual care. Although western culture holds college degrees and ordination in high regard, there is no biblical basis for believing that they qualify us for service. Jesus used simple, uneducated people to work miracles of healing and raise the dead. There's no reason why we shouldn't follow that example today.

One fear we have is that of suffering discipline for praying with a patient. I had that fear and it proved to be unfounded. I'm not saying you won't catch some flak from your supervisor – it's certainly possible. But for citizens of the US, our constitution guarantees certain rights that we don't surrender when we come to work.

I don't advocate a militant or defiant attitude toward prayer in health care. Romans chapter 13 tells us to respect the authorities placed over us and that includes supervisors at work. Humility and a spirit of cooperation will go a long way. God opens doors and changes people's hearts. I do a lot of prayer in the area of asking God to grant me favor with people as I step out in faith and pray for the sick. If God wants you to heal your patients, He'll make the way safe, though you'll almost certainly encounter a little opposition.

I had a dream about this situation shortly after I began praying for my patients. In the dream, I was on the run from the enemy and took refuge in a hospital. I wore scrubs and blended in with the staff. I slept in a bedroom on the top floor where the doctor's dorms were located. I was there for many days. Occasionally an agent of the enemy showed up at the hospital looking for me. When I saw them, I'd pull a surgical mask over my face and duck down a hallway or get on an elevator. As long as I didn't draw attention to myself, the enemy didn't notice me. This was a dream of major revelation. It was God's way of telling me that I was protected and given favor in the setting in which I worked. I could pray for my patients with confidence as long as I didn't make a scene or draw attention to myself. I think we're a lot safer than we believe in the realm of praying for our patients and I believe God will reveal strategies to overcome obstacles if you ask Him.

I'd encourage you to pursue God's heart for your situation. Ask the Lord if you're supposed to be praying for your patients. Begin looking for opportunities to test the waters. When you start praying with patients, expect to see a few miracles. But don't be discouraged if you don't. It was only through months of praying that I started to see people healed. The nature of our job doesn't always allow us to follow up with patients. Some people are healed immediately, but they don't realize it until being tested. Some are healed weeks or months later. Don't give up. God is faithful. He will honor your obedience, in time.

CHAPTER SEVENTEEN

Deliverance

BEFORE LAUNCHING INTO THIS CHAPTER, I'd like to clarify one point. I consider "demons" and "evil spirits" to be essentially the same thing. For writing purposes, I've used these words interchangeably. I believe the Bible also uses them interchangeably. But when I'm with someone who needs to have one removed, I always refer to it as a spirit, not a demon. The term "demon" (in my culture) has the tendency to frighten people, while the word "spirit" is much less frightening.

In 2011, I asked God to teach me more about deliverance. I was in the midst of writing this book and I felt I didn't have much experience to write from. I wanted to understand it better, so I would have some useful information to share. Be careful what you ask God for. He likes to give us things, and they seldom come wrapped in nice, neat packages. I want to take you back to the beginning of my Christian life and show you the path I've taken to get to my present understanding of deliverance.

After being saved, I lived a pretty ordinary life as an evangelical Christian. I was content to study my Bible, sit in my church pew on Sunday and occasionally witness to strangers about Jesus. To my knowledge, I'd never met anyone who was demon-possessed and I'm certain I'd never met a demon face to face. So naturally I didn't understand the preoccupation some people had with demons.

Were these people deceived by an over-active imagination, or were demons really all around us? And if they are all around us, why can't everyone see them?

If there was one thing I sincerely hoped had ceased with the passing of the early church, it was all this messy business about casting out demons. As with everything supernatural, at that point in my life, I was skeptical about the need for studying the behavior of demons, much less casting them out of people.

Most of the experiences we recognize as "real" involve things that happen in the physical world. For those who confine their lives to the physical realm – angels and demons and their strange activities are seldom thought of. The happenings of that otherworldly place are mostly ignored. The problem with demons is that most of us can't see them and for most of us, seeing is believing. Our society has conditioned us to label anyone claiming to see things we don't as suffering from hallucinations. And yet, isn't it interesting how often Jesus dealt with demons and those who were harassed by them?

Demons are disembodied spirits. They don't possess a physical body as we do, but a spiritual one. They interact both in the spirit world and in the physical, although their ability to interact in the physical world is limited. The fact that demons have no physical body compels them to attach to one if they find an opportunity to do so. (And they are *always* looking for opportunities – which should be kept in the forefront of your mind as you read this chapter.)

In 2009, I had a dream that revealed something about demons I didn't know. In the dream I walked the hallways of a hospital and I looked into one patient's room after another. I saw a black presence in each room. I knew the presence was a demon of sickness. Although I don't see demons like this while I'm awake, God revealed an important truth to me through this dream. Sickness is perpetrated by demons and demons are more prevalent than I suspected.

The ability to sense the presence of demons is not available to most of us for a reason. That reason is illustrated in the following story, told by a friend who is a seer. A *seer* is someone who receives revelation from God in the form of visions and dreams (see 1 Sam. 9:9). A seer will often see into the spiritual realm, which is invisible to most of us.

My friend and his six year old granddaughter, who are both seers, were riding in the car when the girl saw an elderly woman hunched over, pushing a shopping cart. The girl noticed that the woman had many demons clinging to her, making it appear as if her hunched over condition was due to the weight of the demons. She asked if they could turn the car around and help the poor woman.

If we were able to see demons clinging to people everywhere we went, but had no power to do anything about them, it might drive us to the brink of insanity. This might surprise you, but if you could see into the spirit world, you would see spirit beings (both good and evil) literally everywhere you looked. But because God is merciful, He hides demonic activity from those who don't need to see it. The ability to discern the presence of spirits is a gift from God given on a need to know basis (see 1 Cor. 12:10). Most of us don't need to know about demonic activity because we aren't engaged in warfare against them.

God has a plan and a purpose for everyone. Each person's purpose comes with some unique assignments. You are free to accept or reject the purpose of God for your life. If you accept an assignment to battle demons, you'll be given the ability to recognize their presence. The presence of demons can be discerned through any of the five senses as well as an intuitive type of knowing.

My Experiences

My introduction to the world of the demonic actually began many years ago, when out of curiosity, I started interviewing patients who reported hearing voices. For years, whenever I transported a patient with a mental health problem, particularly if they were diagnosed with schizophrenia or psychosis, I asked if they heard voices and what the voices told them. I would then ask if they knew who the voices were. The answers surprised me at first, but about 80% said the voices belonged to demons. Many of my patients said that at some point the voice had revealed its identity to them. These people had no reason to lie about their experiences. The likelihood that all of them were wrong seemed unlikely. I had to consider the possibility that maybe I was wrong. After interviewing hundreds of patients, I began to understand that demons were more active than I realized.

One day on my long drive home from work, I had an open-eyed vision. During most of the visions I've had, my eyes have been closed, but this one was different. I saw into the spirit world with my eyes wide open, while I was driving my car. In the vision, I saw myself responding to a call at Tacoma General Hospital for the transport of a woman who was demonized. She was in the emergency department in room number four. I saw myself transporting her to St. Joseph's hospital for mental health treatment.

The next day at work, I responded to a call to Tacoma General Hospital to transport a young woman to St. Joseph's mental health unit. She was in room four in the emergency department. She had no history of mental illness and was being treated for what the doctor called "acute psychosis." According to her mother, she experienced a sudden change in behavior. For some reason she became obsessed with telling everyone about God, angels, demons, Satan, the approaching judgment, and the torment of hell. Her "witnessing" about these things was random and had no continuity of thought. The only recent change that might have contributed to her behavior was that she admitted that her boyfriend had convinced her to smoke marijuana for the first time. This poor woman had come under the control of a spirit of religion. Evil spirits have specialties, which we'll discuss shortly. I have to assume that her experimentation with marijuana was the thing that opened the door for the evil spirit to come into her life. I'll admit this is an assumption, which may or may not be true, but there was no other plausible explanation available and the timing of the two events seemed too precise to be a coincidence.

I transported another woman who suffered the same symptoms. This woman was a middle-aged Christian. We were called to her church to transport her for a mental health evaluation after she suddenly began ranting about God, Satan, angels, demons, the coming judgment and the torment of hell. Once again, her statements were completely random and without continuity of thought. This time I recognized that she was under the influence of a religious spirit, so I attempted to cast it out of her. The more I commanded the spirit to leave, the louder her witnessing became. The yelling became so loud that it concerned my EMT partner and since I was making no progress I gave up.

I've had a number of experiences where members of my family were being harassed by demons. When my son was swimming competitively, I prayed with him frequently for healing of aches and pains. One day he came home with a partial separation of the AC joint in his shoulder, which caused a lot of pain. We prayed and it was healed. Weeks later he told me about a pain he had in the middle of his back. I commanded it to leave and he immediately felt better. But the following day it returned. I was curious, so before commanding it to leave, I closed my eyes to see if God would reveal anything and sure enough, in a vision, I saw my son standing before me with a black creature about 12 inches in diameter attached to the middle of his back. The pain was caused by a demon. I commanded the demon to leave and after it did, I commanded the pain to leave. It left and didn't return.

I've also seen co-workers attacked by evil spirits. While working in Tacoma, my EMT partner was healed at least a dozen times. In the two years we worked together, he was healed of headaches, neck pain, back pain, knee pain, a nasty injury to his hand and numerous other injuries. One day he was complaining of knee pain that was bad enough to make him walk with a limp. I began to command the knee to be healed as usual, but nothing happened. After four or five tries, the pain wouldn't budge. That surprised me, since knee pain usually responds quickly to this approach. Then it dawned on me that I didn't command the spirit of pain to leave.

When I take the time to ask God to show me what's going on, He frequently shows me some kind of demon. Because I saw demons so often, I developed a routine of commanding a spirit of pain or sickness to leave. But this time, I didn't. So I commanded the spirit of pain to leave. Next I commanded his knee to be healed. He felt heat all around his knee and in a few minutes it was healed.

One day I transported a young woman from a fitness club who was hysterical. It took a lot of reassuring to get her calm enough to tell us what her problem was. My partner and I put her in the ambulance and did an extensive interview. We learned that for the past year, she had been hearing voices in her head. There were at least two different voices, possibly more. The voice that she heard most often was a male voice that continually threatened her. The threats involved killing her sister. The second voice sounded exactly like her sister. Often while the male voice was threatening to kill her sister, she heard the second voice screaming in terror as if her sister was being killed. I referred her to a friend who had a deliverance ministry, since I knew virtually nothing about deliverance at the time.

Soon enough, my education about demons became personal. One evening I was praying for my wife to be healed of neck pain, which was so severe it left her in tears at bedtime. I had been praying for her healing for months, to no avail. That night I did something foolish, which you should never do. In desperation, I asked God to put her afflictions on me, if it would take away her pain. I went to sleep and had a dream. In the dream I was walking through a shopping mall looking for something I couldn't find. When I came out of an elevator, the dream suddenly came to an end. This is a classic type of dream that God gives to people who are searching for answers.

I awoke from the dream and a few seconds later I felt something like a net being spread over me. Seconds later, I realized that I couldn't move my arms or legs. All I could do was roll a bit from side to side. As this happened, I also became aware that my voice was being taken away from me. I tried to speak but no words came out. I was aware that what had gripped me in this paralysis was a demon. As my voice left, I tried to say, "Get out, in the name of Jesus," but I could only mumble. My rolling back and forth woke up my wife, who heard me mumbling. She immediately knew it was a demon that had overpowered me and began praying in tongues. She then commanded the demon to leave. A few seconds later my voice returned and the paralysis left.

We later learned from John and Mark Sandford's book, *Deliverance and Inner Healing*, that attacks from paralyzing spirits are common. When I shared my experience on Facebook, I received at least a dozen confirmations from friends who experienced similar attacks. They reported being paralyzed to some degree and most felt a strangling sensation or a loss of their ability to speak. Most people reported that the attack came early in their spiritual life. All of them reported that the spirit left at the mention or thought of the name of Jesus. The mistake I made was asking God to put my wife's afflictions on me. In doing so, I gave the demon permission to attack me and the paralyzing spirit was happy to pay me a visit, since I had agreed with its agenda. Never ask God to give you the afflictions of someone else and never under any circumstances invite sickness or affliction into your life.

I shared these stories to illustrate one thing: demons are real and the more you become involved with them, the more they become involved with you. I never imagined how savagely they can attack us. Contrary to what you may have heard, they can attack Christians. They come in many different varieties and they have different abilities and areas of specialization. Many of us have been taught that the only way a demon can interact with a human is for it to "possess" our body and assume control over us. While violent demonic possession has been popularized in movies and books, the truth about demons and how they operate is far subtler.

Demonic "Possession"

Contrary to popular belief, demons rarely take complete control of an individual. The English Bible descriptions of individuals who were "possessed" by demons are a mistranslation. The term "demon-possessed" isn't found in the Greek text of the New Testament. Instead, three other terms are used. Some passages say "to have a demon." Others say, "to be in a demon." The most common term used is "demonized." These terms mean essentially the same thing and are used interchangeably in the account of the man with the demon named "Legion" (see Mt. 8:28-34; Mk. 5:1-20; Lk. 8:26-39). None of these terms indicate total ownership or control of an individual. They simply mean that the person is in some way affected by a demon.

All the examples from the Bible involving demonic attack describe people harassed in some way but not completely overpowered or controlled. The single exception is the case of "Legion." This is because it takes many demons to completely possess a human. Demons have limited abilities and one demon alone can only attack its host in a particular area. If you examine both Old and New Testament cases of demonization, you'll find that when only one demon is mentioned, the person under its influence is not completely controlled by it.

In the account of the boy with seizures that the disciples couldn't cure, Jesus made an interesting comment about the nature of demons. When the disciples were not able to heal the boy they asked why:

> *Then the disciples came to Jesus privately and said, "Why could we not cast it out?" So Jesus said to them, "Because of your unbelief; for assuredly, I say to you, if you have faith as a mustard seed, you will say to this mountain, 'Move from here to there,' and it will move; and nothing will be impossible for you. However, this kind does not go out except by prayer and fasting."*
> MT. 17:19-21

Jesus said the kind of demon they encountered did not come out except by prayer and fasting, implying that there are different types of demons. Some teachers dispute this, saying that when Jesus said "this kind" He wasn't referring to "kinds" of demons, but rather the "kind" of unbelief the disciples had.

In this verse, the word that is translated "kind" is the Greek word *genos* from which we get the English word "genealogy." This word describes differentiation between related varieties of living beings – specifically between families, races, tribes or nations. It is unreasonable to think that Jesus was describing different families or races of unbelief. He must have meant that there are different families or races of demons and the one they encountered was somehow different.

If you're curious to know how this demon was different from others, consider this: Mark's account mentions that the demon caused the boy to be deaf and mute. Matthew notes that it caused him to have seizures. Both accounts mention only one spirit. This is the only spirit mentioned in the Bible that caused more than one type of physical affliction. It was indeed a different type of spirit (compare Mt. 17:15 and Mk. 9:25).

Demonic Manifestation

When a spirit creates an effect on a physical body, such as trembling, muscle twitching, convulsions or vomiting it is called a *manifestation*. As demons are revealed, it's not unusual for them to manifest in bizarre ways. Some people report sensations of pain moving to different parts of their body before a spirit leaves them. When a demon manifests, it can make the person shake violently or make their arm or leg bend in unnatural ways. It is not unusual for people going through deliverance to vomit a slimy substance. Demons will often speak through the person they inhabit. The individuals often report that these experiences are like being a back-seat passenger in their own car.

On a trip to Australia, I was praying with a woman who wanted to be healed of diabetes. Shortly after I began praying, she reported pain that she didn't have before. The pain was in her back, near her left shoulder blade. I commanded the spirit of pain to leave and the pain moved higher in her back, near the top of her shoulder. I explained to the group that the spirit was moving around in an attempt to confuse and frighten her. A few more people joined us in prayer. We commanded the spirit to leave. It moved to her other shoulder and the pain became worse. We continued commanding the spirit to leave and eventually, it departed. This same woman had just prayed for someone else who had received a remarkable healing of back pain and muscle damage to her leg. And all the while, she had a demon herself and didn't know it.

When praying with someone, if they suddenly experience pain they didn't have before, or if a present sensation of pain moves to another part of the body or becomes worse, it's a sure sign that an evil spirit is manifesting. Demons sometimes manifest to frighten their host. If the demon can create enough fear in the mind of its host they may ask you to stop praying for them, thinking you're only making things worse. My advice in these cases is to tell them there is a spirit present and the increased pain is a tactic it's using to frighten them. Ask if you may continue and reassure them it will eventually leave.

Sometimes demonic manifestation can become so bizarre that it causes problems. There are two schools of thought on this. One belief was popularized by the Pentecostal church. It teaches that when we allow demons to manifest or speak, we give them an opportunity to draw attention to themselves and this is undesirable. The thinking is that we don't want to give the enemy a platform to speak from. For this reason, many people teach that you should not allow demons to manifest or speak and when they do – the manifestations should be ignored.

The other school of thought is that demonic manifestations can help the process of deliverance. One problem with deliverance is that many people refuse to believe they have a demon. One way to convince them is to command the demon to manifest. When the person experiences uncontrollable movements of their body, they quickly realize that their demonic problem is real and they're more likely to cooperate with the process of removing them. Another reason to consider having a demon manifest is to verify whether one is still present or not.

Many people who operate in deliverance work under the assumption that a demon has left simply because they told it to leave. They believe that demons must leave because of their authority, but they never bother to find out if a demon is still there after commanding it to leave. Many times the person who was "delivered" continues experiencing the same symptoms after their "deliverance," because the demon never left. One way to verify the presence of a demon is to command it to manifest after you think it has been removed. If the person still exhibits signs that the demon is present, you'll need to continue the process until it no longer manifests when you command it to.

Demons Specialize

God's creativity is seen in all of nature. No two snowflakes are identical, and no two people are exactly alike. The same is true for demons. They are unique and they all have certain weaknesses, strengths and abilities. Each demon is a specialist in one or more areas, bringing its own brand of affliction to man. This differentiation or specialization is what Jesus was referring to in the passage we discussed earlier in the chapter. Some demons specialize in physical affliction, as with the woman who had been crippled by a spirit of infirmity for eighteen years (see Lk. 13:11), or the deaf and dumb spirit that also caused seizures, which we just mentioned.

Some demons specialize in emotional trauma, like the spirit that terrorized King Saul with what might be diagnosed today as anxiety attacks (see 1 Sam. 18:10).

Some specialize in divination, as was the case with the spirit Paul cast from the woman who followed him for many days (see Acts 16:17-18).

James and John became influenced by an evil spirit when they suggested they should call down fire from heaven to destroy the Samaritan city that did not receive Jesus. Hearing their idea, Jesus rebuked them, saying, *"You do not know what spirit you are of"* (see Lk. 9:54-55). The Lord told them they had become influenced by an evil spirit, which planted this idea in their minds. When we look at the words Jesus used when referring to the way the spirit influenced James and John, the phrase that is translated "are of" is the Greek word *este* which could better be translated "belong to." The phrase "belong to" carries the connotation that one thing has taken possession of another. Jesus said His disciples "belonged to" or were speaking under the influence of this demon, even if it was only momentarily.

Another example of demonic influence of a disciple of Jesus is found in the sixteenth chapter of Matthew. Jesus asked the disciples, *"Whom do men say that I am?"* Peter confessed that He was the Messiah – the Son of God. Jesus commended him saying that His Father had revealed this truth to him (see Mt. 16:16). Later, Jesus began to teach that He would be handed over to the Jews, killed and raised on the third day. Peter rebuked Him, saying these things could never happen. Jesus said: *"Get behind Me, Satan! You are an offense to Me, for you are not mindful of the things of God, but the things of men"* (see Mt. 16:22-23).

Why did Jesus refer to Peter as Satan? Because Peter, like James and John, had briefly come under the influence of an evil spirit. Jesus was speaking to the evil spirit behind Peter's words. If you don't believe that disciples of Jesus can have demons, here are examples of three disciples who did and they were the three that Jesus trusted most.

As we've seen with other accounts of demonic attack, the evil spirits did not exert complete control over them, but only influenced them in its area of specialty. Each of these people remained in control of their mental faculties, apart from the demon's area of specialization. Though Saul suffered anxiety, he had no physical ailments. The woman, who was physically crippled by a demon, had no mental or emotional infirmity. Peter, James and John did not manifest demonic activity or physical illness, neither did the woman with the spirit of divination. Each retained their own identity and did not exhibit signs of complete control by the evil spirit.

The man with "Legion" was a different story. He had lost control of both his mind and body. He was unable to dress himself and couldn't control his own actions, even when put in chains. He mutilated is own body (see Mk. 5:5). He wandered into the wilderness and refused the company of family and friends. When he was asked his name, he couldn't recall it. He took on the identity of the demons that had overpowered him, calling himself "Legion."

As to whether believers can be possessed or harassed by demons, as we've just seen, even Peter, James and John were subject to demonic influence. Jesus himself was attacked and harassed a number of times by Satan. It is unbiblical to believe that anyone is immune from demonic attack. The real issue isn't whether Christians can be influenced or demonized by evil spirits. There is ample evidence from scripture to suggest that we can. The real question is to what degree we can be influenced by them and how does it happen?

Demonic Access

Demons gain access to us through attitudes that reside in our hearts. The apostle Paul warned believers in Ephesus not to allow Satan to use their anger against them, because it provided an opportunity for the enemy:

Do not let the sun go down while you are still angry, and do not give the devil a foothold.
EPH. 4:26-27 NIV

In this passage Paul equates anger with a place of opportunity where the enemy can gain control over our lives. Paul's point that anger provides a foothold for the enemy is illustrated in the case of James and John. The demon that influenced them was able to do so because they became angry at the Samaritans. When we allow anger or other ungodly emotions and attitudes to linger in our hearts, they provide opportunities for the enemy to gain control over us.

Demonic Homes

If demons enter our lives through footholds, they see us as a kind of home. We need to understand not just how they enter our lives, but how they operate once they arrive and how they are removed. Let's look at what Jesus taught about this in Luke chapter 11:

> "When a strong man, fully armed, guards his own house, his possessions are undisturbed. But when someone stronger than he attacks him and overpowers him, he takes away from him all his armor on which he had relied and distributes his plunder... When the unclean spirit goes out of a man, it passes through waterless places seeking rest, and not finding any, it says, 'I will return to my house from which I came.' And when it comes, it finds it swept and put in order. Then it goes and takes along seven other spirits more evil than itself, and they go in and live there..."
> LK. 11:21-22, 24-26 NASB

Jesus likened an evil spirit to a strongman who is armored and keeps his home. He went on to say that when one who is *stronger* comes (a representative of God's kingdom) he removes the demon's armor and evicts the demon from the place he calls home. He said that once removed, the demon may return later if its home remains intact.

There is a widely taught doctrine concerning this passage that needs to be de-bunked. I was taught that whenever a person is delivered from a demon, they need to be filled with the Holy Spirit immediately, because if they aren't, the demon will return. This sounds logical, and the idea of demons returning is certainly illustrated in this passage, but if you look closely, there is no suggestion that the presence of the

Holy Spirit prevents demons from returning. The Holy Spirit isn't mentioned anywhere in this passage. Being filled with the Holy Spirit is always our goal. But many Christians who are filled with the Holy Spirit are in need of deliverance and that need often follows them to their graves. In the last year alone, I've prayed with hundreds of Christians for various problems and most of them had a demon of one kind or another, which had to be removed before their healing could be completed.

In the passage above, Paul said that anger provided a foothold for the enemy. Anger is an attitude that must be dealt with if we are to remain free of demonic influence. But it isn't the only one. Others are rebellion, unforgiveness, bitterness, lust, pride, greed, and the list goes on. Each of these attitudes can allow a place for the enemy to gain a foothold and for a demon to influence us if it specializes in that area.

I had sought healing for chronic neck pain for a long time. I would receive prayer and the pain would leave temporarily, only to return. One day, a woman praying for me asked if I had anger toward anyone. God showed me in a vision a person I had been angry with for a long time. I knew that I needed to let go of the anger I had toward him. When I released the anger to God, the pain in my neck immediately left and never returned.

The anger I held onto served as a foothold for the enemy. When someone would pray with me for healing, the spirit of pain would leave, only to return because it still had a "home" in my life through anger. The solution came when I realized that even though I didn't value this person very highly, God did. That truth destroyed the foothold of the enemy. I no longer had a right to be angry and I forgave him and repented of the anger. This destroyed the evil spirit's "home." When the spirit tried to come back it had no place to return to.

Interviewing Demons

Steve Harmon has been a great help to me in understanding how demons operate. He has years of experience in deliverance and has developed a process for getting to the root of demonic oppression.

Steve compares his method of deliverance to the way a police officer interrogates a crime suspect. He asks the demon a battery of questions to discern how and when the demon entered the person, what rights it has to be there, what other demons are present and how they got there. This is where the ability to see and hear in the spirit realm becomes extremely important.

Steve acknowledges that demons are not always truthful. Interviewing them takes a bit of discernment, but it's worth your time to go through the process because you can uncover helpful information by asking the right questions. Steve found that rather than tell outright lies, demons tend to exaggerate the truth or mix in misleading information. Some of the information they give is useful, such as how and when the demon entered the person and what legal rights it has to be there.

Legal Rights?

Every society has a set of laws upon which it operates. Our man-made laws were derived from spiritual laws that existed long before we created our legal system. This might be a topic for another book, but let me point out that God is a judge and Jesus is an attorney (see Psalm 50 and 1 Jn 2:1). If the spiritual realm has a judge and an attorney, you would expect it to have a court and laws by which it functions. There are rules that exist in the kingdom of God which spirits must abide by. The issue of what legal rights a demon may have over an individual is highly controversial. There are several schools of thought on the matter. Some teach that all legal rights a demon might have to a born-again believer were removed at the cross. Others believe that demons do in fact have legal rights, which we give them – generally when we come into agreement with their agenda and their area of specialty, although other things can give demons legal rights. Steve has interviewed hundreds of demons about how they gained access to their host. He notes that demons are extremely legalistic. They know and understand the eternal spiritual laws that most of us are ignorant of. Demons are always looking for legal loopholes that grant them access to an individual.

The most common reply he has heard when interviewing demons is that they take advantage of individuals during a time when they're vulnerable – often at a young age when they don't know how to cope with a traumatic event. The events typically cause rejection, fear or some other unhealthy feelings. Demons see these events as an opportunity to gain a foothold. A demon will suggest a set of lies that explain what is happening to the person. Not knowing any better, they agree with the demon's assessment of the situation and accept the lies as fact. In doing so, the demon gains access to the person's life through the legal power of agreement. If a demon has gained access through a person's agreement, it usually cannot be removed until the agreement is broken. Here's an example of how a demon might gain access and how it can be removed:

We all have an emotional need to be loved. Accepting the love of our heavenly Father is the best way to have this emotional need met. An unmet need for love creates an opportunity for a demon specializing in lust or pornography to enter our life. (Lust and pornography are the enemy's counterfeits to the Father's love.) If a demon can convince us that using pornography is a way that we can feel loved, our agreement creates a legal right for the demon to influence us. It also creates a home for other demons specializing in that area. Knowing they have a home, demons of lust and pornography will take up residence and begin to influence us.

In order to remove the demon's home and legal rights, the individual must understand how much they are loved and accepted by their heavenly Father. The awareness of God's love fulfills the unmet emotional need. Once the unmet need is fulfilled, the person is now empowered to renounce their agreement with the enemy's lies and repent of their attitude toward lust and pornography. Once this is done, the demons can be safely removed since their home has been destroyed and their legal rights have been taken away.

Most root causes of demonic oppression can be dealt with in this manner. The process looks like this:

1. Identify the root cause.

2. Once the root cause is identified, replace it with the truth from God's heart.

3. Assist them in embracing God's truth, renouncing agreements with the enemy, and repenting of any attitudes stemming from the root cause.

4. Remove evil spirits operating in that area of specialty.

Deliverance Before Physical Healing

Sometimes, an individual needs deliverance from a demon that causes addiction or emotional problems. But there are other times when a person needs to be set free of an evil spirit before they can be physically healed. Let's look at a passage where Jesus removed a demon before bringing physical healing:

> *Now He was teaching in one of the synagogues on the Sabbath. And behold, there was a woman who had a spirit of infirmity eighteen years, and was bent over and could in no way raise herself up. But when Jesus saw her, He called her to Him and said to her, "Woman, you are loosed from your infirmity." And He laid His hands on her, and immediately she was made straight, and glorified God.*
> LK. 13:10-13

This passage contains of number of principles worth noting. First, the woman was bound by a spirit of infirmity, which afflicted her physical body, causing her to be bent over. In this case, Jesus did not confront the demon or command it to leave. He simply said to the woman, "You are set free from your infirmity" and the demon left. We don't know with certainty why He didn't address the demon. It's possible that His mere presence may have caused the demon to leave. After the woman was freed from the demon, He laid His hands on her and healed her deformed body. We can see that she still needed physical healing after the spirit left because she was still bent over. There are two lessons to remember from this passage. The first is that a person may need to have a spirit removed before they can be physically healed. The second is that we should not assume healing has occurred simply because we've cast a spirit out. After it is removed, the person may still require physical healing.

Knowing the Name of a Demon

It is not always necessary to know the name of a demon in order to make it leave. But there are times when it may be necessary. Every demon is different and each situation is unique. For this discussion, let's look again at the case of Jesus and the demon named Legion from the eighth chapter of Luke:

When he saw Jesus, he cried out, fell down before Him, and with a loud voice said, "What have I to do with You, Jesus, Son of the Most High God? I beg You, do not torment me!" For He had commanded the unclean spirit to come out of the man. For it had often seized him, and he was kept under guard, bound with chains and shackles; and he broke the bonds and was driven by the demon into the wilderness.

Jesus asked him, saying, "What is your name?"

And he said, "Legion," because many demons had entered him. And they begged Him that He would not command them to go out into the abyss.

Now a herd of many swine was feeding there on the mountain. So they begged Him that He would permit them to enter them. And He permitted them. Then the demons went out of the man and entered the swine, and the herd ran violently down the steep place into the lake and drowned.

LK 8:28-33

The point I'd like to make from this passage is that Jesus told the demons to come out of the man but they didn't come out immediately. When they resisted He asked for their name. Once the demons told Him their name, a negotiation took place about where they would go when they left. The demons asked not to be sent to the abyss, but rather to be allowed to enter the herd of pigs. Once Jesus permitted them, the demons left the man.

Jesus represents the epitome of walking in full authority. You would think that every demon would be forced to do what He says when He says it. But in this passage while it's clear that the demons feared Him, for some reason they did not obey Him immediately. They wanted Him to tell them where they would go before they would leave. The point of this discussion is to suggest that if Jesus faced resistance from demons it's likely that we will too.

Steve Harmon shared his personal experiences on his Facebook page and allowed me to publish them here:

There was a time when I didn't feel it was necessary to know the name of the demon, until one night. It was a cold and rainy night and we were on our way to pray for a friend, driving on the freeway. Suddenly my girlfriend started to feel dizzy and nauseous. Then her legs started hurting so badly that they felt like they were being crushed. Then her head started hurting. I knew this was a demonic attack. I put my hand on her and commanded healing. She could feel power and heat come off my hand but the demon would override it, making it ineffective. Her vision started to go black and white and she was about to pass out. I prayed for ten minutes and nothing worked, not even a little. I told her to start worshiping. That didn't work. I told her to speak her identity in Christ over herself. That didn't work. I told her to plead the blood Christ over herself. That didn't work. I put my hand on her stomach and released joy on her. She felt joy come off my hand but the demon literally suppressed it.

This went on for 25 minutes and nothing was working. I felt completely power-less. I told infirmity and trauma to go and nothing worked. I said, "Demon leave," several times and there was no progress at all. Through this whole time, I'm asking God for help, but I heard nothing. I thought to myself, "Jesus calmed the storm by living from rest." So, I calmed down. Once I was at rest, I put my hand on her and spoke peace into her. She felt peace come off my hand, but the demon suppressed it. I didn't know what to do. I did everything that I had ever been taught through all my training in deliverance. I parked the car to the side of the road and sat there. All of sudden, I hear the Lord speak to me and say, "It is witchcraft and it was put on her." Immediately I turned and said, "Witchcraft – come out!" Instantly, she felt something move in her body. The demon left within 20 seconds and she was totally healed.

Another time was when I was praying for somebody and I was commanding healing and nothing was working, it was the same scenario. I sat there and didn't know what to do. Then the Lord gave me the word of knowledge and I said, "Parasite, come out in Jesus' name." All of a sudden my friend ran to the sink and coughed up something and he was healed instantly.

I had another situation where the person was having bad lower abdominal pain. I prayed for two hours for healing and nothing worked. I commanded witchcraft, parasite, sickness and tons of other names to leave, but nothing would change. It was 12 midnight and I was tired. I felt bad because I couldn't pray anymore. I laid on the couch and then a word came into my head, "Death." I said, "Death come up." This person said, "It just moved." Then I got another word, "Sorcery." It moved again. All of a sudden I was full of energy and back in the game. I commanded "Death" to come up. I asked death how many demons there were. He said, "Five." I Said, "Name them." He said, "death, sorcery, sickness, word curses, and insomnia." I said to death, "Where do you want to go? The feet of Jesus or the abyss?" He said, "The feet of Jesus." (For some reason, demons choose that option the most.) I said, "I'll send you there if you kick out the four other demons that you are in charge of. If you do that, I'll send you there." The demon agreed. The first four demons came out easy and then I told death to go and the person was completely healed right then.

There were times when Jesus told the demon to leave without getting its name and the demon would go. Then there were times when Jesus would first call out the name of the demon and then it would it go. He would say, "Deaf and dumb spirit, come out," "Unclean spirit," or "Legion." The thing is, with some demons, having its name allows you to assert more of your will over it, breaking its power. But just because you get the name of a demon that doesn't mean it will come out easily every time. It will only come out easily sometimes. Other times it will take longer and in some cases, getting its name won't matter.

Final Thoughts

When I'm praying with someone for the removal of a demon, I speak in a very quiet tone of voice. This may be due to the fact that I do most of my deliverance in hospitals and nursing homes. In these public settings, I can't very well yell at the top of my lungs while I'm telling a demon to leave and I don't think it's really necessary to yell at evil spirits. They're not removed by our tone of voice or volume. They're removed because they have no reason to stay.

Some demons will flee at the sight of a spirit-filled believer approaching. Other demons will fight tooth and nail to remain attached to their host. Demons, as I said, can be extremely legalistic. They know their rights and some of them exercise their rights extremely well. No matter how good our discernment is, some types of demons always seem to evade our ability to detect and remove them. Contrary to popular belief, demons do not want to be exposed. They want to remain concealed. Once a demon is exposed it can be removed. The craftiest demons are extremely good at hiding so they can remain with their host. Our task is to develop a greater ability to discern their presence, discover why they are there and evict them. Because demons are partly responsible for disease, some diseases will not be healed until a demon has been detected and removed. These demons present the greatest challenge to those of us who take deliverance seriously. In some cases it may be wise to use a team approach and have team members relay to one another what they are detecting in the way of demonic activity. In order to walk in the fullness of God's commission we must become competent in delivering people from the oppression brought by evil spirits.

CHAPTER EIGHTEEN

Raising the Dead

So FAR OUR FOCUS HAS been on healing and deliverance, but you must have noticed that raising the dead is included in the commission Jesus gave to His disciples.

Why should we raise the dead? Ask yourself why Jesus raised the dead and why the Father raised Him from the dead. The apostle Paul wrote, "If Christ was not raised, you are dead in your sins." The gospel hinges on the resurrection. The resurrection, as a sign, is unique to our faith. The rest of Christianity can be argued and explained away, but when the dead are raised, the unbeliever, if he is honest, must admit there is a God in heaven who does such things. There is no other explanation.

While many Christians have preached the gospel, very few have tried to raise the dead, even though these two commands are found in the same commission. Many people aren't even aware that resurrections are still happening today. David Hogan is a minister to Mexico and Latin America. Heidi Baker ministers in Mozambique. Both have witnessed over 100 resurrections through their ministries.

While a few Christians have had success in raising the dead, most of us have not. As with healing, when people fail repeatedly at something, it causes them to believe God isn't doing it anymore and they give up. Just as with healing, I believe it is God's will for us to raise the dead and I think there are things we can do to increase our success. Objections and problems with raising the dead once again revolve around the question of whether or not we can know God's will about specific individuals. To help clarify the issue, I'd like to take a look at the four different perspectives we must take into account when we discuss raising the dead.

The Will of the Enemy

As we've noted previously, Jesus said the enemy came to steal, kill and destroy. The enemy wants us dead. One reason God would have us raise the dead is because the enemy wants to kill as many of us as possible and at times, he kills some of us prematurely. Resurrection is how God restores people who die prematurely so that they can accomplish the purposes He has for them.

Family and Friends

The most common scenario for raising the dead is when one of your friends or family members dies. When a loved one dies, it's natural to wish they were still with us. The sense of loss we feel can be overwhelming. If you find yourself in a situation where most of the friends or relatives support a resurrection, the decision is easy to make. But if the majority are not in favor, the decision will be more difficult. While you might have it set in your heart that a deceased friend or family member needs to be resurrected, if others have accepted their death as God's will, your attempts to raise them will create problems. Consider whether the chance of a resurrection is worth the alienation that may result.

The Will of The Departed

We must also consider the will of the person we're trying to raise from the dead. We need to know whether or not they actually want to come back once they've stepped into eternity.

Many valuable insights into the workings of eternity have been shared by people who have died and returned to life after their death. These experiences, which are often called "near-death experiences" (or NDEs) are a fascinating source of information about why people return to life after death. The term "near-death experience" is a misnomer. It suggests that these people come close to death, but narrowly avoid it. But this is not the case. In nearly all of these experiences the individual suffers clinical death. Their heart stops beating, they stop breathing and brain death begins. There is nothing "near" about their death. They are as dead as any other body that has died. A more accurate term might be "life after death experience."

Because I have a fascination with what takes place in eternity, for years I've been asking my patients who have returned from death what they remembered. About 90 percent who remembered the experience said they were given no choice about returning to earth. They had to return because it wasn't their time to die. They died prematurely. The others were usually interviewed by Jesus, and asked if they wanted to remain in heaven or go back. In these cases, their request to return was granted.

I've prayed at the bedside of many cancer patients, who were declared by their doctor to be "terminally ill." In visions, I've seen clear indications that their time on earth was done. Some of these patients were fairly young. I would caution against making the assumption that everyone who dies, whether young or old, can be raised from the dead. Each of us has an appointed time of departure and I think it is wise to consider that some people will prefer eternity over coming back to earth.

The Will of God

Knowing the will of God is critical to raising the dead. He has reasons why some of us will return and why others won't. The will of God in regard to whether or not someone should be raised from the dead does not need to remain a secret. The Bible says:

Surely the Lord GOD does nothing, unless He reveals His secret to His servants the prophets.
AMOS 3:7

The key to knowing God's will about whom to raise from the dead and how to do it lies in receiving prophetic revelation. The needed information can come in many ways. It may come in a dream or a vision, it might come through an angel, a word of knowledge or word of wisdom. Seeking information from trusted prophetic sources may be the best strategy for knowing the mind of God. He may indicate who is to be raised from the dead and how it should be done.

Many resurrection testimonies contained detailed instructions from God on what to do. In a few cases the individual was instructed to lie on top of the body and breathe into it (see 2 Kings 4:34). In others, they were told to massage the hands and feet of the deceased. Some of these suggestions may be hard for you to imagine yourself doing. Bear in mind that friends, family members and employees of the facility may be shocked if they see you doing these things. If you're led to do something that would cause people to object, take whatever steps are necessary to do them discretely.

Whatever you ultimately decide to do – it should be done in faith, believing that God is going to raise them back to life. Remember the words of Jesus to Jairus, "Do not be afraid; only believe, and she will be made well."

Once we have permission to proceed with a resurrection, we must face the incredibly poor likelihood of success. Sometimes the resurrection will happen, but most of the time, it will not. The question people often ask is, "Why?"

Some would point to a lack of faith or the presence of unbelief as the main reason for failed attempts at resurrection. These are possible explanations. Just as with healing, we need to develop confidence in God's ability and desire to raise the dead before we'll see it happen consistently. Another problem is that we might be praying for someone to return, not knowing that they have no need or desire to come back. Each of us has a set of appointed tasks to accomplish here on earth. Some of us may accomplish our tasks before we reach old age. If we die after completing the majority of them, we may have no reason to return

The difficult question is whether we should attempt to raise the dead every time we have the opportunity, or if we should ask God for His will in each case. Prophetic information is desirable, but it's not always available or 100 percent reliable. I'd like to address this question by drawing from illustrations about what I've experienced in my practice as a paramedic. There are principles we use in medicine that can be applied to raising the dead.

Protocols

In the world of emergency medicine we have different ways of managing patient care. Some treatment requires us to contact a doctor to ask their advice on what to do. If I'm at a car accident with multiple patients who have various types of injuries and I'm not sure where they should be transported and what treatment to provide, I'm going to ask for help. I'll get a doctor on the phone and get their direction on how to proceed. The doctor advises me where to transport the patients and what treatment to provide during transport.

But some situations are so time-sensitive that a delay of even a few minutes to talk to a doctor could prove fatal. For these cases, we've developed *protocols* to manage the way in which patients are treated. We memorize treatment protocols and deliver the same care in every case. These situations are ones that we rarely see and they're serious enough that a mistake in judgment could cost someone their life.

Management of cardiac arrest is an example where our actions are guided by protocols. When stress and confusion might prevent us from making the right decisions, we develop a planned response based on best practices in the past. When everyone involved knows the protocol and does their part, the events are less stressful and there's little question afterward about whether the team did the right thing. Protocols tend to remove our emotions from the decision-making process, allowing us to operate in a less stressful environment, with less concern about making mistakes.

Another reason we use protocols is because we deal with patients who aren't able to tell us their wishes. Sometimes we merely transport them to a hospital, but other times we attempt to bring them back from the dead. We rely on what is referred to as "implied consent," which is the assumption that if the patient were able to communicate their wishes, they would want to receive every treatment available to save their life. In the event that someone doesn't wish to be resuscitated, they fill out a form and have it witnessed by a doctor. The form specifies which treatments may be done and which are withheld.

Todd White was asked if we should pray for everyone or only the ones God wants to heal. Todd believes that God wants to heal everyone. When someone objects on the grounds that not everyone we pray for is healed, Todd's reply is, "Show me the person Jesus didn't die for, and that's the one I won't pray for." Todd is an example of a person who operates from a type of protocol.

Asking Permission

Not everyone believes that we should always pray for healing or a resurrection. Some people believe we should ask God for permission first. They generally point to the words of Jesus when He said He did nothing but what He saw the Father do (see Jn. 5:19). This view causes them to pursue only the healing or resurrection that God specifically authorizes. I have a friend named Sue Wilke, who has been used by God to heal people. Sue is forever having conversations with the Holy Spirit. Wherever she goes, she hears His voice directing her to this person or that one. Sue always asks permission and because she hears Him so well, she gets detailed instructions on how to pray for each one.

Earlier in the book, I shared the dream Ken Nichols had where Jesus gave him authority to heal anyone he wanted to. Ken operates from a kind of protocol because he was given instructions by Jesus to operate that way. Sue has no use for protocols, because she's been trained to hear from God. I fall somewhere in the middle. I like to approach strangers with confidence, knowing that God will back me up if I want to see someone healed, even if I haven't asked for His permission. But I frequently seek revelation from Him in the midst of praying, because it helps me get to the root of the problem and remove it.

Should we use protocols in healing and raising the dead, or should we seek God's heart in every case? I think there is ample room for both positions. Some of us will ask permission, because we hear God clearly and we like getting His take on things. Some of us will pray for every deceased person because we're convinced it's always God's will to raise them. In the end, we all need to obey the revelation God has given us. The only thing Jesus asks is that we are faithful to what He tells us. We don't need to obey the revelation someone else has. We need to obey the revelation we have.

Examples

You might be wondering what it would look like to actually raise someone from the dead. The possible scenarios are nearly endless. A common setting for a resurrection is where a believer witnesses a stranger die suddenly and they quickly bring them back from death by praying or commanding them to come back to life. These individuals, after coming back, often go about their life without much trouble and with no need for the believer to become personally involved in their life other than to explain what happened.

If you're trying to resurrect a friend or relative, you can simply sit beside the body and pray as you are led the Holy Spirit. The process might take hours or possibly even days. Heidi Baker's team might pray for 24 hours before they re-evaluate whether or not to continue. Sometimes when the person comes back to life there is little that would cause you to take notice that they are alive. Some of the signs of life can be hard to detect. Look for signs of breathing like the rise and fall of the chest. If the person does in fact come back from death, you should notice small muscle movements. As time goes by you will probably notice more of them. Dead bodies don't normally move except in a few extremely rare situations where physiologic changes occur as the body decomposes. If you notice movement, it is probably a sign that the person has come back to life. The resurrection of a dead body can happen slowly or quickly. Some people come back to life and appear just as active as they were before they died, but some take more time to regain normal activity.

If you want to raise someone from the dead after a day or more has passed you may have to explain to morgue attendants and funeral home employees what your intentions are. You will probably need to obtain permission from the family and the facility before proceeding. Once you have permission from everyone involved, you can sit near the body and pray as God leads. How long you pray is up to you and the facility. They will probably not allow you to stay after the close of business at the end of the day, but there's no reason why you can't continue praying at home.

A well-known resurrection testimony came out of Nigeria where a pastor named Daniel Ekechukwu was raised from the dead three days after he died. After being pronounced dead by a doctor from injuries he sustained in a car crash, his body was taken to a morgue and embalmed. His wife received permission to place his coffin in the basement of a church where Reinhard Bonnke was preaching. During Bonnke's message, two men who volunteered at the church noticed movement coming from inside the coffin. They removed Daniel from the coffin, alive and well. While this testimony might sound hard to believe, all the people involved have been interviewed and their stories support this testimony. Two doctors, the ambulance driver, the morgue attendant and the church volunteers all reported that Daniel died, was embalmed and was raised from the dead after three days.

If you work in a hospital you may encounter deceased bodies regularly. Your approach may be as simple as speaking to the body or the dead person's spirit and commanding them to come back to life. At times you may need to ask a family member if they'll allow you to pray for a resurrection. In a testimony that came from St. Francis Hospital in Federal Way, Washington, an emergency department doctor and nurses prayed for the resurrection of a deceased patient. After being without a pulse for 45 minutes, the patient came back from death with normal brain function.

On occasion you may find yourself attempting to resurrect a complete stranger. Depending on the setting, the person who is raised from the dead may have no clothing, no food and no place to stay. It might be wise to plan for these problems in advance and find a safe place for them to stay and if needed, someone to care for them. The person who comes back from death may need extensive care for a period of time. I've read testimonies from people who were healed of the injuries or illness they died from. But I've also read testimonies where they were not. After returning from death, the person may require months of hospitalization to recover from illness or injury. These people usually need emotional support and they may incur expenses that they'll need help with. Consider ways in which your friends or your church might help them.

We'll close this chapter with a quote from my Facebook friend, Terry Mengle:

Thirteen years ago my wife and I met a young man from Africa who explained that in his country anyone who wanted to graduate from Bible college must raise someone from the dead. They would go to where the dead awaited burial and command the dead to rise. They made attempts until the dead were resurrected and then they graduated and were ordained to go and minister for Jesus.

CHAPTER NINETEEN

Proclaiming the Kingdom

BEFORE BEGINNING THIS CHAPTER, I would like to clarify one point. The four gospels use two similar terms: the "kingdom of God" and "the kingdom of heaven." While there may appear to be a difference between these two terms, the gospels use them interchangeably and I will use them to refer to the same concept.

As Jesus healed the sick, raised the dead and cast out demons, it was His custom to proclaim the glad tidings of the kingdom of God. The healing power of God has a message attached to it: "The kingdom of God has come near you."

> *Now it came to pass, afterward, that He went through every city and village, preaching and bringing the glad tidings of the kingdom of God. And the twelve were with Him.*
> LK. 8:1

Divine healing is not primarily about physical health and wellness. The main objective of healing is to confirm a message from God. The message is that God wants to re-establish a vital and living relationship with mankind. The relationship we might have with Him was broken by the effect of Adam's sin as noted by the apostle Paul:

> *Therefore, just as through one man sin entered the world, and death through sin, and thus death spread to all men, because all sinned.*
> ROM. 5:12

The sin of Adam not only caused separation from God, it was also the reason death entered the world. Atonement for sin was made through the shedding of blood by animal sacrifice. But the blood of bulls and goats could not provide a sacrifice for all mankind and for all time. So at the appointed time, Christ came and the shedding of His blood on the cross made possible the reconciliation of all mankind.

Therefore, as through one man's offense judgment came to all men, resulting in condemnation.

> *Even so through one Man's righteous act the free gift came to all men, resulting in justification of life. For as by one man's disobedience many were made sinners, so also by one Man's obedience many will be made righteous.*
> ROM. 5: 18-19

This message of reconciliation to God and eternal life is good news to those who don't know it yet. This message is known as the *gospel*. Although reconciliation to God and redemption from sin are at the heart of the gospel, there is another aspect that we should be aware of. The gospel is the revelation of God's kingdom.

The kingdom of God is perhaps the most elusive subject in all of Scripture. Views on the kingdom are many and varied. Some people see the kingdom as something that is entirely future. Some believe the kingdom is at hand today. Some see it as purely allegorical and others see it as literal. Some see the kingdom as a fulfillment of the promises God made the Jews, while others believe it has nothing to do with Jews.

Some believe it pertains only to the heavens themselves, while others believe the kingdom has an earthly presence.

Although there is disagreement over the totality of the kingdom and its fullest expression, it seems that at least part of the kingdom must be a present reality on earth. Jesus indicated that the kingdom was something we should seek to enter (see Jn.3:5). He also taught His disciples to pray that God's kingdom would come and His will would be done on earth in the same way it is in heaven (see Mt. 6:10). Therefore it seems that it must have at least some fulfillment in the present age. And it is this aspect – the *present* manifestation of the kingdom of God on earth that I would like to discuss in this chapter.

In the Sermon on the Mount, Jesus recognized that we all have needs, such as what we will eat and what we will wear. He noted that we often worry about God's willingness and ability to provide for our needs. He illustrated the Father's willingness to meet our needs by drawing attention to how the birds are fed and lilies of the field are clothed according to God's goodness and abundance. He then told the crowd to trust in the Father's ability and desire to meet their needs because they were more valuable than the birds or lilies. Finally, He revealed how our needs can be met, saying, "Seek first the kingdom of God and His righteousness and all these things will be added unto you." The way in which we receive the abundance of the Father is by seeking and entering the kingdom of God (see Mt. 6:25-34).

On October 12, 2010, I had a dream about the kingdom of God that illustrates this reality. In the dream, I watched as different people experienced the kingdom. The first man lived as a drug addict and petty criminal. He lived in a perpetual state of fear, always keeping an eye out for the police who might catch him doing something wrong. He lived to have his own personal desires met. It was a life of fear, selfishness and using others. Then I saw him enter the kingdom of God.

I saw him dressed in a uniform as he sat on a stool at the opening in a wall. The wall stood as a divider between a prison cell and the kingdom of God. The opening in the wall was a gate about four feet wide. He was a guard at this gate. He got up and walked around in the kingdom, which seemed to be an endless expanse as far as the eye could see. As he explored this new place, he looked for familiar things but found nothing like what he experienced in the world. There were no crimes or drugs and no police. Everywhere he went he experienced freedom. He could walk anywhere without nagging feelings of fear or guilt. He was never afraid of getting caught doing something wrong, because nothing wrong ever happened in the kingdom. All his needs were met and he was filled with peace.

He met God the Father who had only good things to say about him. The Father provided everything he needed in the kingdom. He went back to the stool and sat at the gate. His new calling was to tell those who asked how they could enter the kingdom. His life was profoundly changed by his experience. Although the daily problems of his life didn't immediately disappear, he began living from the reality he had experienced in the kingdom. The freedom he felt there allowed him to live free in the world. In the dream, he never lived in fear again.

I was also in the dream. In the world, I was looking for acceptance and to be understood by others. I sought popularity and wanted people to like me. That was, until I entered the kingdom. In the kingdom, I found immediate acceptance. Everyone I met seemed to instantly understand me. Even more amazing was the fact that they liked me. I had no enemies and made friends everywhere I went. When I met the Father, I encountered absolute acceptance and love. He had many wonderful things to say about me. I was the apple of His eye. Everything I did was perfect in His sight. He could not be more proud of me. In the dream, this experience profoundly changed how I lived in the world. I no longer went around seeking acceptance from others. I lived from the reality I had experienced in the kingdom and never again wondered if I was good enough.

A third person appeared in the dream. This person lived with the fear of never having enough money. Although he had a good job and invested his money wisely, he lived with a nagging fear of poverty. Thoughts about earning and saving money plagued him continually. This man also entered the kingdom of God.

In the kingdom, he traveled from place to place. Wherever he went, he noticed that no one worried about money. In fact, there were no worries of any kind in the kingdom. Citizens of the kingdom had piles of money. He found that he could easily get as much money as he wanted from any stranger on the street. Nobody hoarded money. No one cared about how much they had or how much they gave away. There was abundance for everyone. This experience in the kingdom profoundly changed the way he lived. Experiencing the provision of heaven and knowing that God's economy never lacked resources, gave him a freedom with money he never thought possible. In the dream, his fear of poverty instantly vanished. He began living in the world from the reality he had experienced in the kingdom and began to give abundantly and with gladness.

A major theme in this dream was God's abundant love and acceptance. The second was His abundant provision. The third was His righteousness, where no crime was allowed. The kingdom is a place of perfection. Those who experience the perfect realities of the kingdom are able to live in this world from those realities, instead of the ones the rest of the world lives from.

Jon Sellers is a Facebook friend and gifted teacher on the kingdom. I like the way in which he explains the kingdom of God and how it is to be proclaimed. He has graciously allowed me to share some of his observations:

> Historically one of the problems in understanding the kingdom has been a focus on spatial concepts in thinking about God. This has led to confusion about where heaven is, where God is, where Christ is, and it's led to a failure to grasp the reality of our lives in the kingdom of God, now.

> The kingdom of God is perhaps best understood as a new relationship under the rule of Christ the King, rather than a realm that we journey to or a period of time during which Jesus will reign over the earth.

> Jesus lived as a supernatural man. Although He is God, He divested himself of His own power and authority and operated under the anointing of the Holy Spirit, just as we do. Our goal is to become like Him. It is the relationship we have with Christ in the Spirit that opens us up to the revelation and experiences of the supernatural. It is only the transforming presence and power of the Holy Spirit that enables us to walk like Jesus did. To walk in the Spirit is to

have a relationship with Him. This is why I believe relationship is preferable to realm in thinking about the kingdom of God.

The scriptures draw us continually into relationship. Even the kingdom of darkness is not so much a realm as it is the absence of proper relationship under the rule of God. The enemy is in rebellion to God and therefore is not in His kingdom. He has been cast out. Does this speak of realm or relationship?

The whole world is under the power of the enemy. Is God absent? No. He is present always and everywhere. But the whole world is in rebellion and is not in the kingdom. God is not without power and influence in the world now; the entire universe is upheld by Him. But He has allowed rebellion and so the call to come into the kingdom is primarily a call to turn from that rebellion and to turn to Him in faith and obedience. This enables us to receive all the riches of Christ. We are seated with Him in heavenly places. Do these things speak of realm or a relationship?

If God is present then it must be that to be seated with Christ in heavenly places is to be properly oriented to God in Christ as the representative man, the second Adam. We share in the obedience of Jesus Christ who is now at the right hand of God and in us at the same time by the Spirit. Because He is at the right hand of God, we have also gone behind the veil into the holy of holies, because we are in Him.

When Jesus talked about the kingdom of God, He was not primarily referencing the spiritual realm, nor was He specifically referencing the realm of God's presence, where He dwells, where the angels are, where He has prepared mansions for us. When He said the kingdom of God is within you, it is best understood as 'among' you. The kingdom first is represented to the disciples as the person of Jesus. He is the King and the one in whom they saw the kingdom. Then as the disciples were called and followed Him, and as the multitudes followed Him, the kingdom grew.

The disciples were given power and authority because they entered the kingdom and became representatives of the king. They have been given authority to do what Jesus did as part of the ongoing ministry of expanding the kingdom until the glory of the Lord covers the earth as the waters cover the sea. We are each called, commissioned, tasked and empowered to do the same things until He returns.

There seems to be confusion in the body of Christ over what preaching the gospel of the kingdom should look like. This confusion is partly due to the differences in how Jesus and the apostle Paul presented the gospel of the kingdom. One area that is perhaps not spoken of enough is how the Jewish people understood the gospel as Jesus related it. His preaching of the gospel was couched in the language and imagery of the Messianic promises to Israel. The gospel as Paul preached it was a continuation of that but it was couched in terms that explained it for Gentiles.

The major emphasis of the good news of the kingdom of God concerns salvation from sin and reconciliation to God. Salvation as Jesus taught and as Paul taught are not in conflict, but are emphasizing different aspects of it, ultimately bringing the same result. That result was to bring people into recognition of Jesus as the Son of God, Messiah and Savior; to bring them into putting their faith in Him; and to enter into the grace of God, which produces eternal life in Christ.

Both Jesus and Paul performed miracles as signs and as expressions of the reality of the kingdom of God and as expressions of the love and goodness of God. Both pointed out the absolute necessity of believing in Christ. Both called people to repent. Both called for radical transformation of the individual and society. Both healed, cast out demons and raised the dead.

In the gospel of John, Jesus talked about His signs in several ways. He pointed to them so that people would believe in Him. He expected them to believe and when they didn't, He rebuked them. In all of that the clear mission of His coming was to be the Savior of all. The benefits of the kingdom, which tie Jesus to the Messianic prophecies from the Old Testament reveal the heart of God for people now, not just in eternity, and demonstrate that Jesus is the Son of God who is able to do those things as part of God's testimony to Him.

How we proclaim the gospel of the kingdom depends on the dynamic of each situation. We relate to people according to the truth of Christ, who we are in Him, the reality of the Kingdom of God and who they are, their needs and what the situation presents. There really is no formula for proclaiming the gospel. Man-made formulas for evangelism exist because we have failed to love others as Christ did. Love implies relationship and making disciples requires authentic ones. The Holy Spirit should direct the way in which we present the good news.

Jon and I have discussed the kingdom of God often. His perspective has helped me understand my place and function as one of God's representatives. My personal experiences with proclaiming the kingdom have varied greatly. Many times I have simply told the person who was healed, "The kingdom of God has come near you." Sometimes I've said, "God healed you, because He loves you." Other times I've asked what they thought about God after being healed, which can lead to a longer discussion. Each situation is different. Following formulas is problematic, if only because of time constraints. When you have two minutes to tell a stranger about the kingdom, you'll have to use a different strategy than if you have 30 minutes.

I don't endorse the use of formulas like the "Romans road," or asking people to pray the "sinners prayer." While many people like these approaches, the disciples didn't use them. Having said this, I have at times employed one of these methods, but not because it was a habit. It just seemed like the approach God wanted to use with that person.

One day I responded on an emergency call for a woman who was suicidal. After living for years as a prostitute, she didn't want to go on. Depressed, discouraged and hopeless, she cut her wrists in a feeble attempt to end her life. I was called to transport her to the hospital.

As I walked near her, I felt the Holy Spirit's presence come over me powerfully. I knew that He wanted me to minister to her in some way. During the ambulance ride to the hospital I told her she could have a completely new life. This was the good news she had been waiting for. I led her in a prayer to accept Jesus into her heart, to receive forgiveness of her sins and to be made into the new creation that God promised. She wept tears of joy as we rolled her into the emergency room. When we returned an hour later with another patient, we walked by her hallway bed. She reached out, took my hand and thanked me for telling her about God and showing her the path to a new life

To finish this chapter, I'd like to share something written by my Facebook friend, Roger Webb:

> As you read my miracles testimonies that I post, what you do not hear or read is the ministry of the Word. God confirms His Word with signs following.

Years ago while I was conducting revival meetings, I was in my motel room waiting for the night's service. I heard a car door slam in the parking lot and it caught my attention. I looked out the window and saw a man getting out of his car, walk to the back and open the trunk. Being on the top floor I could see the man very clearly. I watched as he lifted something out of the trunk. It was a wheelchair. He unfolded it and wheeled it to the passenger side. I could not see who was on that side of the car. All I could see was the roof. I watched as the man open the door then I saw him bend over and reach in and struggle for a bit. Then I saw that he held a woman in his arms. He put her in the wheelchair.

As I watched the man struggling to lift her, my heart broke. That dear man had to lift her in such an awkward position. I know the man was damaging his back lifting that way, but there was no other way to get her out. Then on top of that, when I saw the dear woman in his arms, my heart broke even more. This dear woman was totally dependent on him helping her.

By this time I was crying my eyes out. What I just witnessed simply broke my heart. As I was crying, I was praying and asking the Lord to release to me power to see miracles that will cause the cripples to walk.

As soon as I prayed that I heard the Lord say something that sank deep into my heart. He said, "Preach something that I can work with. Preach messages that I can confirm with signs following and I will work miracles." I knew exactly what He was telling me. Preach Jesus and lift Him up and He will work miracles that will set the captives free. From that day forward I have strived to keep the messages aimed directly at Jesus and God has done His part. The lame walked, the dead are raised, the deaf hear. Jesus Christ is the same yesterday, today and forever!

CHAPTER TWENTY

Making Disciples

AFTER HE WAS RAISED FROM the dead, Jesus appeared to the disciples and gave them what is commonly known as the great commission:

> *"All authority has been given to Me in heaven and on earth. Go therefore and make disciples of all the nations, baptizing them in the name of the Father and of the Son and of the Holy Spirit, teaching them to observe all things that I have commanded you; and lo, I am with you always, even to the end of the age."*
> MT. 28:18-20

I became involved in a discussion on Facebook with a group of leaders from the street healing movement. Brandon Lee, one of movement's visionaries asked how we might go about making disciples after seeing people healed. Most of us had seen hundreds of people healed on the streets. Some were led to a profession of faith, but few of them were walking in the power and knowledge of God as we had hoped. The question we all wrestled with was, "How do we make disciples?"

Many church leaders don't question the process of making disciples. They lead congregations that meet regularly. They invite non-believers to attend weekend services and occasionally hold community outreach events. They teach the Bible and have small group meetings during the week. The process may have a few more components, but this is a standard model for making disciples.

These activities may bring people to God; getting people to make a profession of faith isn't difficult. But keeping them in a relationship with God afterward is more problematic. Church polls reveal that many new converts leave the church or lose faith in God shortly after meeting the pastor or evangelist. These short-lived conversions don't translate into life-long discipleship. Some church leaders have recognized that present models of evangelism and discipleship aren't working.

The Problems

One problem is the model where a congregation meets in a building once a week to hear one person speak. This model lends itself well to certain things. It's effective for teaching in the broader sense where a message can be heard by thousands of people. But practical application is a different matter. Putting instruction into practical use can't be accomplished in large groups, particularly if feedback is needed. Application must be done in smaller groups to allow for personalization and time for questions to be answered. Congregations that meet once a week have no time for practical application of the principles that are taught. Some churches have developed small groups that meet during the week for this reason.

The commission Jesus gave is extremely practical. It's full of things that need to be done more than once a week. It was the custom of the early church to meet in the homes of believers often. Having frequent contact with others is one key to success in mentoring. The more often you have contact, the more opportunities there are to reinforce the things needed for growth. And making disciples is a growth process.

The leaders of the street healing movement have identified some problems with the present church model and have proposed some changes. This has put them at odds with leaders who have no desire for change. Many of the leaders of the street healing movement are young and on fire for God, which accounts for their extreme enthusiasm and willingness to scrap traditional practices. They've rejected the broken paradigm of their fathers in favor of a new model for their generation.

They've seen the effects of powerless preaching and the weakness of a Church body sitting in a pew on Sunday lulled to sleep by sermons. They have a vision of a Church that's different – a vibrant, spirit-filled, demon-casting, sickness-destroying, dead-raising army of disciples who do the things Jesus did. They know that this vision will never become a reality without leaders to point the way, train people, and encourage them on this path. This vision requires leaders who have a different mindset.

They've seen that one of the main problems is church leadership structure. Looking at how leaders function, they've identified a system that establishes different levels of authority. This hierarchical model is present in nearly all of Christendom. As much as Protestants complain about the papal structure of the Catholic Church, most protestant denominations have a structure that looks no different, where priests, bishops and cardinals are replaced by worship pastors, youth pastors and senior pastors.

This structure emphasizes and draws from the gifting of one or two people who lead the congregation. It rarely allows for the development of the gifting of the congregation itself. Among fellowships where gifting of the congregation is developed, it seldom deviates from the gifting of leaders and is seldom allowed to surpass it.

This structure facilitates certain things that the Church needs to accomplish, but it's not effective for making real disciples. And it's this issue that leaders of the street healing movement are most concerned with.

The kingdom of God is transformational. It breaks mindsets that are opposed to the righteousness of God. It frees people from bondage to sin and empowers them to release the miraculous into the lives of others.

The kingdom is not a set of precepts we agree to, it is the transformational power of God working in the lives of believers, changing them into the image of Christ. In a span of three years, Jesus took uneducated men and transformed their lives by using frequent demonstration and teachings on the kingdom. When the process had done its work their lives replicated the life of their teacher. This is the goal of making disciples; it's the replication of the kingdom of God in the lives of others.

One of the problems of our Christian culture is that it's easy to live as a part-time Christian. Many of us have little interaction with other believers outside of Sunday church services. We tend to compartmentalize our Christianity, bringing it out only when it's convenient. On Sunday we put on Jesus, but He remains hidden the rest of the week.

The spiritual growth necessary to be transformed into a disciple is an ongoing process. It happens little by little through daily renewing of the mind. As we meditate on new revelation from God and obey the leading of the Holy Spirit, our perceptions, beliefs and actions take on new directions. As we get together with other disciples and operate in the power of God, faith for the miraculous grows.

After becoming a Christian, I attended a Bible-teaching church for seven years that had a congregation of almost 1,000 people. I'm a social person, but in all those years I never really got to know one person in this Church. I learned the Bible backward and forward, but I was spiritually dead and knew nothing about how to operate in the kingdom of God. I'm a textbook example of how the Church is great at making converts, but often fails at making disciples of Christ.

The Solutions

Having experienced this failure, God asked me to try something different. Through several dreams He led me to a few kingdom-minded people and I began the process of becoming a disciple. I didn't even know it at the time, because the ones doing it never called me a disciple or treated me like a novice. It was a very natural process. I found a few people who knew more than I did and they were very willing to entertain my questions and help me grow in spiritual maturity. Almost none of this occurred inside of a church building. Much of it was done by e-mail, through blogs, over the phone and on Facebook. Welcome to the world of electronic discipleship.

As I mentioned, Nor'west Prophetic is one of the men who took me under his wing. I had a dream in which he and I walked the streets of the town we lived in. In the dream, we were starting a new type of Church called a "Missional Church." We were looking for a person of peace. Finding this person was the first thing we had to do. Once again, I'd like to draw your attention to the instructions Jesus gave His disciples in Matthew chapter 10 and Luke chapter 10.

In His instructions, He told the disciples to go out into the cities of Israel. The first thing that should be obvious is that He didn't tell them to bring people to a central location, as we do today. His instructions were for them to go out into society. He also told them to inquire who was worthy and then to find a person of peace. He told them not to go from place to place, but to remain there, eating what was served, healing the sick, raising the dead, casting out demons and teaching them about the kingdom.

What is the emphasis in these instructions? Developing relationships while ministering to people and teaching them about the kingdom.

The person of peace is the key to the entire process. The *person of peace* is a person who sees the work that God is doing through us and is willing to receive this same work in their own life and potentially, the lives of others. The person of peace desires to build a relationship with us. That relationship requires trust and a spirit of peace. Once this person is found, they may lead us to a group over which they have influence. If we gain favor and acceptance with them, we may gain it with the entire group. Just as we are doorways to the kingdom, the person of peace is a doorway to the world. The work of God flows through these doorways.

Biblical examples of a person of peace are numerous. The gospel came to the Gentiles after an angel spoke to Cornelius, who was called a "just man of good reputation." The angel told him to send for the apostle Peter. Cornelius allowed Peter to speak to all who were in his home and the Holy Spirit fell upon them. Cornelius, by virtue of his reputation and influence, served as the first doorway for the gospel to reach the Gentiles. He is one of the clearest examples of how a person of peace facilitates the work of the kingdom (see Acts chapter 10).

Lydia is another example, having opened her home to Paul and the disciples after receiving their testimony (see Acts 16:14-15). The Samaritan woman at the well likewise took the message of the Messiah back to her city after meeting Jesus (see Jn. 4:28-29).

One example might surprise you. The man with the demons, who called himself "Legion" became a person of peace. Some people are by nature a person of peace. Some become one as a result of our interaction with them. This man was a citizen of Gadara. Once he was set free, he begged Jesus to allow him to remain with Him. The people of Gadara begged Jesus to return to Galilee. Jesus sent the man home to Decapolis to tell of the great things the Lord had done. Later, when Jesus visited Decapolis, the people there begged Jesus to stay and touch their sick and infirmed. The man's testimony prepared the hearts of people so He could return (see Mk. 5:16-20 and Mk. 7:31-37).

When John G. Lake trained his divine healing technicians, he sent them to the home of someone in the community who needed healing of a terminal condition. The household would have had at least one person willing to cooperate with the work that God was doing. They would pray over this person and their household, focusing on getting the sick person healed. They would teach the Bible and mentor them as long as needed, which would have been anywhere from a day to a few months. This model, which proved to be very effective, is almost exactly like the one Jesus gave to His disciples.

If you haven't been exposed to the House Church, Organic Church or Missional Church movements – you might benefit from checking them out. God is doing some good things in the way of making disciples through these expressions of His Church. They may not be experts in healing, but they're extremely good at making disciples. The common thread running through all of them is their emphasis on the concept of *being* the Church, instead of *going* to church. If this concept seems strange to you, it's likely that you identify the church as a place instead of a group of people. The Bible identifies the Church *(ecclesia)* as the body of disciples who follow Jesus and not a place where we meet.

The focus of these groups is on the incarnation of Christ in us, and the expression of His life through us in a continual way, not just one or two days a week. They emphasize frequent fellowship with other believers.

It was after I decided to be more intentional in allowing Jesus to live through me on a daily basis that I noticed changes in the lives of people around me. Those who were never interested in my religion were very interested in the healing they began to hear about. Those who never cared about Bible study were interested in learning what God was saying to them through dreams. The further I walked into the kingdom, the more people were attracted to Jesus. And my opportunities to disciple them increased dramatically.

Making disciples is a matter of practicing a few key things consistently. You must find a person of peace and develop a relationship with them. If they open doors to the lives of others, ask God how you can meet their needs. You must have regular contact, demonstrating Jesus in His power, forgiveness, love, compassion and all the things that reveal His life in you. If we do these things, we will make disciples and fulfill the great commission. And in the process we'll reveal the truth that Jesus is still alive and breathing in those He calls His bride.

CHAPTER TWENTY-ONE

Persistence Pays Off

ONE NIGHT I HAD A dream in which I was praying for a number of people over different periods of time. For some, I prayed for several days, for others it was weeks and for others I prayed for months. Some of my friends knew I was doing this and criticized me for it. But their criticism didn't stop me. In the dream, I knew I was doing the right thing, so I kept praying.

For many people, prayer consists mostly of asking God to fulfill their needs or desires. Their prayer never goes beyond asking and hoping to receive. These individuals tend to see God as the sovereign Lord over all creation. They believe that nothing happens outside of His perfect will. Not knowing His will, they would never presume to know the outcome of their prayers in advance. These believers might be offended by Christians who presume to know the will of God and pray as if they have authority over their circumstances.

Another group of believers operate on the premise that God has given them authority over the power of the enemy. They see God as their Father who has delegated responsibility, power and authority to them and knowing His will, they seldom ask God for anything. Their prayers are more like the declarations of a military officer involved in warfare. They contend for things already promised by God as an inheritance they possess. Many people in in this group can't justify begging God to act on their behalf and they get frustrated with people who do.

In the realm of healing, I've noticed that the second group seems to have better results than the first. Those who *command* healing tend to see a lot more miracles, compared to those who *ask* God for healing. It wasn't until I learned how to pray from a place of authority that I began to see miracles. Today they're quite common.

But I still have a number of people that I pray for who are not healed immediately, or should I say – they show no signs of being healed when I pray. And it's this problem I'd like to address in this chapter.

In the dream, I found myself praying for certain people every day for weeks or even months. Persistence in prayer was the thing God was speaking about. I don't know why some people are healed immediately while others require 30 years of prayer and still others die without being healed. But I think it's worthy of a discussion. Someone once asked Todd White why God doesn't heal amputees. Todd's reply was, "How many amputees have you laid hands on?"

I think Todd was proposing the real reason why more people aren't healed. It's not because God doesn't want them healed. It's because we don't want them healed enough to spend hours, days, weeks or months praying if that's what it takes. We often blame God for not healing people when the blame probably belongs to us. We expect immediate results and if we don't see an instant change, we give up.

If you endeavor to operate in healing, you'll eventually find a person who requires prayer over a long period of time. They may have multiple sclerosis, Lou Gehrig's, autism or Lyme disease. Whatever their illness is, they will find you. And when they do, your persistence in prayer is the only thing that will get them healed. I believe many more people would be healed of such diseases if we would learn to persist and not give up so quickly.

If you're in need of healing and you're wondering if it's foolish to ask for prayer over and over again, my advice is to keep asking as long as it takes to get healed and don't ever give up. In Luke chapter 11, after teaching His disciples how to pray, Jesus taught them how to persist until they received what they asked for. Bethel Church recently saw a woman healed of multiple sclerosis after she'd been in a wheelchair for 30 years. I would imagine she'd received thousands of prayers over the years and nothing ever changed, until the day that one last prayer tipped the scales in her favor.

I have many friends who are leaders in the current healing movement. Although they're as different as can be when it comes to styles and methods of healing, they all share one thing in common. Every one of them has remarkable persistence in prayer. Though they all pray for people who are not immediately healed, these setbacks don't affect their ability to keep praying for hours or days if that's what it takes to get someone healed. Their determination and persistence is the thing that sets them apart. They are leaders partly because they are successful. Their success comes from persistence. If you want to have the same kind of success they have you must develop the same kind of persistence they have.

CHAPTER TWENTY-TWO

Receiving Our Healing

IN THIS CHAPTER WE'LL DISCUSS the various problems people have with receiving healing from God. As I thought about the problems some of us have with receiving healing, I realized that the process of healing is similar to the way a football player catches a pass from a quarterback. I'd like to draw an analogy from this American sport because I think many principles of the game of football apply to healing, though the analogy isn't perfect.

For those who are not familiar with American football, allow me to briefly explain what's relevant to this discussion. Football is a game in which two opposing teams try to control the movement of a ball on a field. One way the ball can be moved is for one player to throw the ball to another player. The person throwing the ball is called a quarterback or passer. The one catching the ball is called the receiver. There is also an opposing team whose goal is to prevent this from happening.

The quarterback's job is to take the ball, look for a receiver who is in a position to catch a pass and throw the ball to him. Generally, as the quarterback throws the ball, the receiver is running. The receiver's job is to run a pre-determined route, get free of the other team's defender, catch the pass then run with the ball toward the goal line without being tackled by a defender.

The opposing team (also known as the defense) tries to break up this plan. Defenders can tackle the quarterback before the pass is made, knock the receiver to the ground before he can run the correct route, taunt the receiver with intimidating words and when the ball is in the air, try to catch it, or take the ball away after the catch is made.

Good receivers know that a few key things, if done correctly, will improve their ability to catch the ball and hold onto it. Good defenders come armed with a host of tricks they use to prevent receivers from catching the ball.

One thing that drives a quarterback crazy is a receiver who won't run the correct route. The quarterback throws the ball to the receiver as he is running. The speed of the receiver and the delay between when the ball is thrown and when it's caught requires the quarterback to throw the ball in front of the receiver. The quarterback must anticipate where the receiver will be and throw the ball to that spot. Once the ball is thrown, the receiver must continue running the route that will get them to that spot, then locate the ball and catch it. All of this requires precise timing and coordination.

The receiver must do several things, all in quick succession. First he must run the route the quarterback expects, next he must break free of the defender. He must anticipate the timing of the throw, locate the ball in mid-air and follow its trajectory into his hands. Finally, he must hold onto the ball as the defender tries to either strip it from his hands or tackle him.

Some receivers don't run routes correctly. As a result, they don't catch many passes. Sometimes they quit running or run slowly because they're tired or they believe the quarterback will throw the ball to another player. Some receivers are prevented from running the route when the defender hits them. Some will retaliate and hit the defender back. They might injure the defender, but they take themselves out of position to catch the pass.

Some receivers are skilled at running routes, but they don't catch many passes. Poor receivers can be distracted by the defense and are easily intimidated. Some are fearful of what will happen if they catch a pass. At the critical time when the ball is in the air and their eyes should be looking for the ball, they're looking somewhere else, thinking about the defender, or their hands aren't in the right position. If any of these things become a habit, the receiver will be inconsistent. Poor receivers are easily distracted and intimidated; good receivers are fearless and focused.

The Rookie Receiver

As a new member of the team, the rookie receiver is unaware of the things that veterans know, putting them at a disadvantage. In his *favor* is the fact that the opposition usually underestimates the ability of rookies. They focus more on veteran receivers, often putting two defenders on them, leaving a rookie uncovered. This can provide the new-comer with excellent opportunities to catch a few passes without interference from the defense. As a rookie proves himself, he becomes the target of the defense and draws more harassment.

Some rookies rise to the occasion, making catches that surprise every-one including themselves. Determined ones find ways to outsmart and outplay defenders. Instead of being intimidated, they become more determined to win. Their leaping, one-handed grabs and acrobatic catches leave defenders looking like incompetent fools. Quarterbacks dream of having receivers like this on their team.

Many talented receivers succumb to intimidation, pain, and harassment from defenders who battle for every ball thrown their way. Some can't shake the memories of the reception that was rewarded with a hit so hard it required surgery and months of physical therapy afterward. Some see themselves as unable to measure up to the expectations of the fans and the team. When fear or low self-esteem sets in, receivers can develop an attitude of defeat that prevents them from playing up to their full potential.

In summary, good receivers play without fear. Some are unafraid because they don't know the strength of the opponent. Other receivers know the opponent's strengths, but they've learned to outplay them. Receivers who live in fear tend to play poorly. Now let's turn the discussion back to healing.

Fear

I'd like to share a story about someone who wasn't healed the first time I prayed for her. Early one morning in October of 2011, a co-worker made her way outside to wash an ambulance. I noticed she was limping and asked what happened. I told her that I see a lot of people healed and asked if I could try to get her healed.

She said, "What do you mean?"

"I just want to pray over your knee."

With a concerned look she asked, "What are you going to do to me?"

"Can I take a look at your knee?"

She rolled up her pant leg and showed me the swollen knee. I could see her kneecap was displaced laterally.

"I just want to place my hand on your knee and pray."

She asked, "You aren't going to hit me, are you?"

"Why would I want to hurt you?"

She said her roommate intentionally hit her on the injured leg a couple of times and she wanted to make sure I wasn't going to do the same thing. I told her I wasn't going to hit her and she finally agreed to let me pray over her knee. When I did, she felt nothing. I prayed three times with no change. I told her that I believed she would see her healing soon and walked away.

I was disappointed. I really wanted her to be healed. On the same day, I prayed with another co-worker, who had a partially torn Achilles tendon and pain in his back. He was healed of everything instantly. That day and for a few days following, I asked God why one person was healed and the other one wasn't. I believe God told me the man with the Achilles tendon injury and back pain was healed because he gladly received his healing without fear while the woman with the injured knee wasn't healed because she was afraid.

A couple of months later, the woman with the injured knee saw me loading my gear in the ambulance. She came over and asked why she wasn't healed. I told her I believed it was because she was afraid of being hurt and fear prevented her from being healed. I told her the offer was still open. If she wanted to be healed, God would heal her. She said she wanted to be healed. We sat on the couch at our station. She showed me her swollen knee, wrapped in a bandage. I asked God to bring His presence upon her then asked what she felt.

"I feel really relaxed and at peace."

I commanded the swelling, inflammation and pain to leave and commanded the ligaments, tendons, muscles, nerves, cartilage and bones to be healed. She felt heat going through her knee, which increased each of the three times I prayed. While her knee was being healed, I taught her how to keep her healing. (We'll discuss that in the next chapter.) I warned her that the symptoms might return and told her to believe that she was healed and to command the symptoms to leave if they returned.

I saw her three weeks later and asked how her knee felt. She said it felt great. I asked if she was serious. With a smile, she looked at me and said, "Yeah – it feels great!"

When she wasn't healed the first time, the easiest explanation would be to assume that God didn't want her to be healed. That's what many of us do. Thinking that we prayed with faith, when someone isn't healed, we wonder if perhaps God doesn't want them healed. The fact that this woman was healed at a later date demonstrated that the failed healing wasn't a problem with God; it was a problem with her. She could not receive healing in a state of fear. One of the most frequent problems with failed healing is the fact that we can't receive all that God wants to give us.

This is a difficult concept for many of us to understand, particularly if we believe in a God who is all-powerful. God is indeed all-powerful. He is able to do whatever He wishes. But He has chosen to limit the manifestation of His power for healing to that which we're able to release or receive through faith. Our faith, our fear, our doubt and unbelief all play a role in how healing is released and received. It was fear that prevented her from receiving her healing, because fear opposes faith.

In these two examples, the only difference I could see was that one person was open to prayer and had no fear, while the other was reluctant about prayer and was afraid. These attitudes are not uncommon. In fact, they represent two of the most common types of receivers you're likely to meet.

Many people are ignorant about divine healing, the reality of demons, the existence of God and problems of abuse in the church. These people are, is a sense, spiritual rookies, who don't have a reason to be fearful. I've found that they usually receive healing rather easily. While many of them are neutral on the issue of God's existence, they'll agree to let you pray with them because they feel they have nothing to lose. They aren't afraid of God or Christians and they haven't been wounded in the church or suffered demonic attacks. They have a simplistic almost child-like view of spiritual matters. I would liken them to the children whom Jesus said were able to receive the kingdom of God. I've prayed with two such people often in the last few years. One of them is my son, the other is my former EMT partner.

Both of these guys are prone to frequent injury. In the past four years I've prayed with each one over a dozen times for various conditions like neck pain, back pain, knee pain, a partially separated shoulder, headaches, stomach pain and a hand injury. The first time I wanted to pray for healing they were willing to let me try and both were healed instantly. The same thing happened the next time. After that, every time they needed healing they asked me to pray with them because they knew they would be healed. No fear. No doubt. No unbelief. Both received their healing each time I prayed with them.

Their view of healing is simple. They figure that if God healed them in the past, He would heal them again. They've learned how to be good receivers of healing by practicing their receiving skills. The process for receiving healing looks something like this:

- Ask for healing
- Expect to be healed
- Receive God's healing power
- Believe you are healed
- Be thankful for your healing

We all come into the world without views toward spiritual life. Only through experiences, both negative and positive, do we develop things like fear, doubt, anxiety, faith, courage or hope. The experiences we have color our perceptions of God and His ways. Our perceptions dictate the things we think about and the ways in which we think about them.

In contrast to the spiritual rookies, there are those who have had many spiritual experiences – both negative and positive. It's this group, and in particular, those who have had negative experiences that seem to have the most trouble receiving healing. If you've prayed with many people for healing, you've probably noticed a few folks who stand out from the crowd.

Some people are untrusting when you ask if you can pray with them. The fears they have are usually due to negative experiences they've had in the past that they don't want to repeat. The negative experiences involve things that were said or done to them. It's not uncommon to have someone tell you that you're not healed yet because you don't have enough faith. When you hear this repeatedly, it can make you think twice about asking for prayer. I've heard complaints from women who reported being groped by a man who prayed for them. It's for this reason that healing conferences often restrict prayer to team members who have been selected in advance. When prayer includes prophetic ministry, the one praying might believe they have discerned sins the person has committed and announce them publicly. There is no real benefit to exposing someone's sins publicly. When this is done it causes them to suffer shame and condemnation. There are many other ways in which people can be wounded during times of prayer. Someone who has had negative experiences like these can be difficult to pray with simply because the situation of receiving prayer itself can bring back painful memories from the past.

Another type of person is the Christian who has received prayer from many people who are successful in healing, but they still haven't been healed. They may actually seem to be sicker than when they first began. Many of these individuals become obsessed with their medical conditions to the point that it's all they talk about. Most of their conversations are a monologue about how bad their disease is, how doctors have failed them and how many people have prayed with them unsuccessfully. Eventually they'll confess the fear that God doesn't want them healed.

In many cases, the individual becomes fixated on past failed experiences, instead of focusing on seeing themselves healed. As much as they're sick and tired of being defeated, they can't visualize Jesus actually healing them. Some don't believe they're worthy of healing, some feel it's their punishment or cross to bear, and some believe their sickness is a divinely appointed lesson to build their character. For whatever reason, they haven't learned how to be a good receiver of healing.

I suspect that some of these people suffer from demonic oppression that has not been dealt with. Demonic oppression can create fear and hopelessness, which worsens their symptoms and prevents them from receiving the healing they so desperately want. If they were to be delivered of the demonic oppression, no doubt they would probably be healed.

We know that faith is one of the keys for those who desire to release God's healing power. If we have fear, unbelief or uncertainties about God's will in healing, we won't see people healed. These things are barriers to releasing God's power, but they also prevent us from receiving it. As the one praying, we can pray a perfect prayer of faith, but if the one we're praying for is full of fear, they may not be healed.

James reminded the church about the necessity of asking God in faith and not doubting:

> *But when you ask, you must believe and not doubt, because the one who doubts is like a wave of the sea, blown and tossed by the wind. That person should not expect to receive anything from the Lord. Such a person is double-minded and unstable in all they do.*
> JAMES 1:6-8

This instruction was given to the church, to those who know God. We can't expect people who don't know God to ask Him in faith for healing, but we can expect it of the church. I believe it's for this reason that many people in the church have not yet received their healing.

Like the receiver who can't shake the defender, they never seem to be open to receive the pass and when they are, their eyes are distracted as the ball approaches. If they manage to make the catch, the enemy quickly steals the ball, leaving them with another demoralizing defeat. But the cycle of defeat can be broken.

If someone receives prayer from multiple people with a good track record for healing and no progress is being made, it almost certainly points to a demonic presence that hasn't been dealt with. Further prayer for healing without removing the demon(s) will be fruitless. Deliverance should be considered in such cases, if the individual is willing.

Another problem is a mind that hasn't come to accept the reality that Christ is our healer, and that healing is available to everyone, regardless of their situation. It's easy to believe that some people deserve healing more than others. It's equally easy to believe that some deserve sickness more than others. Healing is an act of God's grace. Like any other work of grace – we cannot qualify or disqualify ourselves as a recipient. Grace is given freely to all who are willing to receive it – regardless of our perceived merit. If we believe there is a valid reason for our sickness, our healing will likely not manifest until we understand the truth about God's healing grace.

Our minds must focus on Jesus and the great love He has toward us. We must meditate on his mercy, love, grace and kindness toward us and refuse to entertain thoughts to the contrary. Fixing our eyes on Jesus is the most important step we can take in becoming a better receiver of healing. To bring this chapter to a close, I'd like to share a testimony from my friend Mike Laabs about a dream that provided the key to his healing:

About 10 years ago I developed severe allergies and I avoided going outside from April to August at all cost. My eyes felt painfully dry, my nose was constantly running, even with blood sometimes. It was no fun at all. The doctors gave me medications to get through that time, but each year it got worse. After I was invited to learn about supernatural healing, I commanded that stuff to leave. It was a constant struggle. Half the day it was fine and I could even breathe through my nose, but it always came back.

Two years ago, I was crying as blood came from my nose. I had pain all over my face. I cried out to the Lord, "What's going on, why am I not being healed?" He said to me, it's because I see myself as still being sick.

I was embarrassed and angry. I said, "No way, I know I'm healed by your stripes."

Silence then... so I decided to take a nap and lie down for a while, still crying.

Then I remembered what the Lord said and asked him, "I see myself as sick? What does that mean?"

Suddenly I was in a dream. I found myself walking in the midst of a field with all the triggers I could imagine – without fear of them. I just stood there looking around and all of a sudden I realized how these flowers smelled. In all these years, I forgot how spring smells with all its flowers in bloom. I realized what Satan had taken away from me. I cried, and cried and cried. The dream went on for about 20 minutes. It took me that long in that dream to realize that I really was healed. When I woke up, I was healed!

Mike saw himself as a sick person. Even though he was trained in divine healing, he still believed he wasn't healed and he feared going outside. It was fear of still being sick that allowed the symptoms to persist. Once he saw himself through the eyes of faith as a healed person, his symptoms disappeared and they never returned.

CHAPTER TWENTY-THREE

Keeping Our Healing

IN THE DISCUSSIONS THAT I'VE had with believers who heal the sick, there is much controversy over whether those who are miraculously healed need to do anything to remain healed. The controversy stems from the belief by some that it is not necessary to maintain healing that comes from God. They look at the Bible and see no mention that people healed by Jesus had to maintain their healing. From this they conclude that it's neither necessary nor possible to do it. In this chapter we'll look at what Scripture says about maintaining our healing. I'll also share a dream I had and we'll look at some personal experiences.

I've met a number of people who have experienced healing, only to have the symptoms return a few days later. I've also experienced this myself and so have friends who are used by God to heal others. Roger Sapp, who has prayed with over 25,000 people for healing, estimates that 25 percent of people who are healed experience a return of symptoms.

The evidence seems to indicate that losing the effects of healing is a real phenomenon, even if we don't completely understand why it happens.

One perspective on healing is that if we, as the ones praying, have the right kind of faith, people will not only be healed, but they will remain healed. Adherents to this view believe that a return of symptoms indicates weak faith on our part. They see healing as a mechanical process brought about as our faith releases the power of God. They reject the idea that the sick person has any part in receiving or keeping their healing, putting all the responsibility on the one who is praying. Again, this view is based on the fact that the Bible doesn't specifically discuss whether or not we must do anything to keep our healing.

I'd like to address the absence of biblical instruction on maintaining our healing by comparing it to the absence of biblical instruction on maintaining our salvation, since salvation is more extensively covered and better understood by most of us.

The narrative passages in Scripture tell us that people were added to the church at different times. An example is when approximately 3,000 people were added to the church on the day of Pentecost (see Acts 2:41). We know these people were saved, but what isn't revealed is that all these believers would wrestle with the realities of their salvation for the rest of their lives. Salvation is not just a matter of accepting Jesus as your savior. If you died five minutes after becoming a believer, yes, your soul is saved from the consequences of sin. But if you live longer, your salvation also requires you to maintain your relationship with God. For most of us salvation becomes the ongoing process of being transformed into the image of Christ, know as sanctification.

Those saved on the day of Pentecost were people just like you and me. Some of them would wonder at times if they were really saved. Some would struggle with rebellion against God. Some may have even walked away from God before their death. But the details of how their salvation and sanctification were worked out are not mentioned in scripture because the Bible was not intended to be a biography of their lives. Similarly, the Bible is not a biography that records the details of how people lived after they were healed. If these details had been included we may have read about the same struggles we see today.

If people who are saved do not maintain their relationship with God, do we blame the evangelist? The same question can be asked about healing. If symptoms return after a person is healed is it because the healer wasn't able to keep them healed?

My point is this: If we are going to hold the healer responsible for the continued manifestation of an individual's healing, why don't we hold the evangelist responsible for maintaining their relationship with God?

Most of us understand that we have a responsibility to participate with God in working out our salvation and being conformed to His image. But when it comes to healing and deliverance, we expect that we can sit back and let God sovereignly keep the demons out of our lives or keep us from having sickness and pain. Unfortunately, healing doesn't always work this way. We must start asking what our responsibility is in cases where remaining healed is an ongoing process, as opposed to the one-time miracles, which don't require any further battles.

The Dream

I had a dream that revealed one of the keys to keeping our healing. The dream involved people who were being treated at a hospital for various diseases. As they were healed, they left the hospital and had to make a decision. They had to either leave their account with the hospital open or close it. Those who kept their account open could continue discussing their disease or injury as long as they wanted. They could return for more treatment and discuss the progression of sickness with a doctor or make payment arrangements. These people always became sick again.

The other group decided to close their account after they were healed. They were not allowed to come back for follow up appointments. They didn't talk about their disease or even think about it after being healed, except to testify once in a while about their healing. This group never again became sick. This was the content of the dream.

The dream reveals two mindsets or types of people and how they view and respond to healing. One mindset is focused on sickness and the process of treating it. The other is focused on health and healing itself. The key to keeping our healing is how we view healing and sickness themselves.

Let's examine a passage from Scripture where Jesus addresses the issue of keeping our healing. There was a man at the pool of Bethesda who had an infirmity for 38 years. After he was healed, Jesus caught up with him and shared these words of warning:

> *Afterward Jesus found him in the temple, and said to him, "See, you have been made well. Sin no more, lest a worse thing come upon you." The man departed and told the Jews that it was Jesus who had made him well.*
> JN. 5:14-15

Jesus told the man to sin no more, lest something worse would come upon him. This instruction suggests that sickness can be the result of sin and that our healing might be maintained if we avoid sinful behavior. Since Jesus was the one who healed him, the return of his symptoms would not be a result of inadequate faith on the part of Jesus. It was the man's responsibility to keep his healing. We have the same responsibility today. Notice that the man went to the Jews and testified about his healing. In the dream that I had, those who remained well, were those who testified about their healing. Could our testimony of healing contain a key to remaining healed?

One problem that many of us have is that we love to testify about our sickness. We complain and grumble and tell everyone we know about how bad our condition is. Some of us believe that our ability to put up with our illness proves something about our character. Some people complain to get sympathy from others. And many of us refer to our condition with terms like "my diabetes" or "my cancer." We've seen previously that life and death are in the power of the tongue (see Prov. 18:21). Our words are a reflection of our thoughts. Our thoughts flow from the things that we meditate on in our hearts. The things we focus on are the things we talk about. And that which we talk about we give power to. It is the tongue that holds the power of life and death and it may hold the power to keep us healed. Our words reveal that some-times, we take possession of our diseases and acknowledge ownership of them. Once we take ownership of something, getting free of it can be a difficult process.

Some people I've asked to pray with confessed that they didn't want me to pray with them because they knew if they were healed they would lose their disability check. Others choose to remain sick because they receive attention or sympathy. When we use sickness to obtain something that we want, we become dependent on what it provides and we become slaves to sickness.

Whether it brings money, attention or the opportunity to obtain pain medications, some of us are accustomed to a lifestyle of sickness. We expect to have doctor appointments for the rest of our lives. Healing Rooms Ministry founder Cal Pierce noted that our health care system is more like a disease maintenance system. It becomes the thing around which our world revolves. Some of us are so dependent on this lifestyle that we fear what life would be like without doctor visits and medications. Those who allow sickness to become their lifestyle may have sickness return no matter how many times they are healed.

In the dream that I had, those who continued a lifestyle that focused on sickness always became sick again. Those who refused to talk about sickness kept their healing. Their words and the fact that they refused to focus on sickness helped them to remain well. I'm convinced that one key to keeping our healing is a matter of what we choose to focus on and what we talk about.

Honoring the Body of Christ

There is one more section of Scripture we might examine to learn how to maintain our healing. In 1 Corinthians chapter 11, Paul addresses several things, one of which is sickness and premature death. He begins the discussion in verse 17, with an observation about the behavior of believers toward one another:

But in the following instructions, I cannot praise you. For it sounds as if more harm than good is done when you meet together. First, I hear that there are divisions among you when you meet as

a church, and to some extent I believe it. But, of course, there must be divisions among you so that you who have God's approval will be recognized!
1 COR. 11:17-19 NLT

Paul continues his list of complaints against them:

When you meet together, you are not really interested in the Lord's Supper. For some of you hurry to eat your own meal without sharing with others. As a result, some go hungry while others get drunk. What? Don't you have your own homes for eating and drinking? Or do you really want to disgrace God's church and shame the poor? What am I supposed to say? Do you want me to praise you? Well, I certainly will not praise you for this!
1 COR 11:20-22

Paul then describes how the Lord passed on to him the celebration of the breaking of bread and drinking the cup in remembrance of His death (see 1 Cor. 11:23-26). He then adds this observation:

(27) So anyone who eats this bread or drinks this cup of the Lord unworthily is guilty of sinning against the body and blood of the Lord. (28) That is why you should examine yourself before eating the bread and drinking the cup. (29) For if you eat the bread or drink the cup without honoring the body of Christ, you are eating and drinking God's judgment upon yourself. (30) That is why many of you are weak and sick and some have even died.
1 COR. 11:27-30

It would be easy to assume that Paul was referring to how believers viewed the Lord Jesus when he said they should honor the "body of Christ'" when they eat the bread and drink the cup. But I don't believe that's what he was referring to. In this passage, two different terms are used. He refers to "the body and blood of the Lord" in verse 27, and "the body of Christ" in verse 29. Paul often referred to the body of believers, or the *Church* as "the body of Christ."

In this passage Paul was telling the Church that their behavior toward one another (the body of Christ) was the reason some had become sick and died. Remember, his complaint against them was division, quarreling and selfishness. As he brings the discussion to a close he again emphasizes their behavior toward one another:

> *So, my dear brothers and sisters, when you gather for the Lord's Supper, wait for each other. If you are really hungry, eat at home so you won't bring judgment upon yourselves when you meet together.*
> 1 COR. 11:33-34

In this last section Paul ties the judgment that some people had received (sickness and death) to the fact that they didn't honor one another when coming together. According to Paul, showing honor to others can actually prevent us from becoming sick or dying prematurely.

My Experiences

One night as I went to bed I developed sudden pain in my lower back that radiated down the back of my left leg. I'd never had this type of pain before, but I knew from transporting people with these symptoms, it was consistent with a herniated lumbar disc. The pain was severe and for a moment I panicked, thinking I'd done something to injure my back.

As I thought about the pain, I remembered that God had been speaking to me about pain returning after healing. This was a new concept as I'd only been praying with people for about a year. On a hunch, I took the position in my mind that the pain was not a herniated disc, but an imitation of that pain, caused by a demon. I told myself repeatedly, "I do not have a herniated disc." Suspecting an evil spirit was at work, I commanded the spirit to leave. After ten minutes it left, but it returned 20 minutes later. When it returned I repeated the same process and had my wife join me in the battle. This went on for two hours. Each time we did this, the pain would leave – only to return. Finally, I was so exhausted I had to go to sleep, even if the pain was still there. I decided to rebuke the spirit one last time and commanded it not to return. When I went to sleep the pain was as bad as it had been all night. But when I awoke in the morning I was pleasantly surprised to find that I had no pain – and it never returned.

I learned a great deal from this experience. I learned that we may have the symptoms of a condition that perfectly mimic the condition itself, with no actual injury or disease process in our body. A demon can create a near perfect imitation of a real medical condition. I also learned that a key to victory over the enemy lies in what we believe and what we say. I refused to believe or admit that I had a herniated disc, even though the symptoms felt exactly like it. I also learned that although we might see complete removal of the spirit and symptoms once, it doesn't mean they won't return. And if the symptoms return, the strategy that worked the first time can be used again as often as needed until the spirit realizes we aren't going to allow it to afflict us. I've used these principles in my own life many times since then. Today, when I pray with someone who has been healed, I always try to spend a few minutes teaching them what to do if the symptoms return.

In 2010, I had a chance to help my sister-in-law obtain healing for an occluded artery in her leg. She suffered from poor circulation in her leg for many years. Her foot was always cold and numb and her doctor had been considering placing a stent in the artery to keep it open. One day, I asked if she wanted to be healed and she said yes. I commanded the artery to be open and the circulation to return to normal. She didn't feel anything different until the next morning, when she woke up with a warm foot that had normal sensation and circulation. She was beaming with joy. Later that day, her foot became cold and numb and with a worried heart she asked me what happened.

I sat her down and explained that healing and sickness are a battle between the kingdom of God and the kingdom of darkness. Like it or not – healing is warfare. God wants us to be healed and the enemy wants us to be sick. I'm not sure that my sister-in-law is a Christian, but she understood what I was saying. I told her the enemy brought the symptoms back to try to convince her she wasn't healed and that all we had to do was push back a little and do some more warfare. I commanded her leg to be healed again and a few minutes later the circulation returned to normal. I told her that all she needed to do was to resist the enemy's tactics if it happened again. "If the symptoms return, command them to leave." With a smile of understanding she confidently maintained her healing and she's had normal circulation in her foot since that day.

My sister didn't want to continue the merry-go-round of sickness. She wasn't getting sympathy from anyone. She received no financial benefit. She didn't dwell on how her ability to endure the condition proved that she had great character or strength. She received no gratification from it whatsoever – she wanted it gone. Once she was healed, she chose to close her account with sickness.

She and many others like her will be healed and remain healed, because they earnestly want no part of their condition. Once it's gone, they don't imagine what will happen if it returns. Fear that our sickness will return is an easy trap to fall into. Fear is a tool of the enemy. When we are healed, we are given a taste of God's power and love. The Bible says,

There is no fear in love; but perfect love casts out fear, because fear involves torment. But he who fears has not been made perfect in love.
1 JN. 4:18

When we fear the return of sickness, we do so because we doubt that God has really healed us or that we will remain healed. We may also doubt that He truly loves us. Fear and doubt about God's goodness allow the enemy to bring sickness back. When we live from a place of faith, we walk on ground that God has given us as our possession. It is our inheritance and our refuge. Faith is our place of strength. The enemy is at a disadvantage when we walk on the ground called faith. When we walk in doubt and fear, we walk on the enemy's ground, which allows him to keep us in pain. Where we walk is a choice we have to make. The choice we make determines the outcome of our healing. Fear will keep us in sickness. Faith will keep us healed. This is why we must close our account with sickness and choose never again to entertain these thoughts

Roger Webb shared this testimony on Facebook about how some people view healing and sickness:

I have often wondered just how many people would rather talk about their sickness instead of be healed of their sickness. So many would lose their benefits if they got healed and would rather have the monthly income instead of being free.

I remember a woman several years ago that attended a service. I laid hands on her and she was instantly healed of major knee and leg problems. You should have seen the look on her face when all the pain left and she regained full mobility. She was jumping around so excited!

The next night I was looking for her so she could give her testimony but she was nowhere to be found. Her friend that brought her the night before told me when her friend got home it dawned on her that she was going to lose her monthly check because she no longer had a disability. The woman got depressed and went to bed and woke up the next morning upset. She told her friend she would rather have a monthly disability check than be healed. She went and laid down on the couch and by the time afternoon rolled around all the pain returned and she was right back to her disability and crippled up. She refused to return to the miracle services.

Roger Sapp made this observation about keeping our healing:

I prayed about this matter and felt that the Lord told me that because I was getting them healed on the basis of my faith rather than their faith, this was creating this situation.

In other words, I knew how to stand in faith and receive a healing for them but they didn't know how to stand in faith to keep it. Whatever is received by faith in Christ must be maintained by faith in Christ. When a symptom arose, they quickly doubted that they were healed and didn't maintain it. So today, we spend more time getting them to believe for themselves, helping them deal with their doubts and teaching them what to do if a symptom returns... which is to do the same thing that they did to receive the healing. They had to believe that the healing belonged to them before they received it. They had to believe that Christ had purchased it for them at the cross. Nothing has changed if they have a symptom. They must believe that the healing still belongs to them despite a symptom because of what Christ has done. What causes someone to receive... faith in Christ as Healer... is what causes them to maintain. Today, I think that we have a lot fewer people losing their healing.

In summary, there are a number of things we can do to maintain our healing. One is to treat others, particularly those in the body of Christ, with respect and honor. Another is to avoid sin. It's good to occasionally testify about our healing instead of testifying about our sickness.

We should refuse to entertain thoughts about sickness returning and instead fix our thoughts on God's goodness. Another key is to resist the tendency to take ownership of the condition by referring to it as "mine." And occasionally, if the symptoms return we might need to command them to leave. We must continue to believe after we are healed, that Christ is still and always will be our healer. Once we are healed, we must close our account with sickness.

CHAPTER TWENTY-FOUR

When People Aren't Healed

I'D LIKE TO DEDICATE THIS chapter to the friends who have come to me often for prayer and are still not healed. I want you to know that I haven't given up on seeing you healed. You've received prayer from so many people and you're still not well, but you refuse to quit. Your persistence is remarkable. I've learned some things by talking with all of you and it's my hope that eventually you'll get the breakthrough you're looking for. Thanks for being patient with God as He teaches us about healing. Thank you for not giving up on us.

We're on a journey of discovery. That journey is a progressive revelation of eternal truths that have existed in the mind of God and upon which His kingdom was built long before Adam walked with Him in the cool of the day. On this journey, we'll find many things that have been hidden, waiting for us to find them. For in Christ are hidden all the treasures of wisdom and it is His good pleasure to give us the kingdom. Yes, God has hidden from us the treasures of wisdom. Why, you ask? So that we might pursue them and in the process find Him. Our journey is nothing less than the complete revelation of God and all of His ways through His son, Jesus.

One of the mysteries we hope to uncover has to do with the question of why some people are healed while others are not. Some may be content to shrug their shoulders and say, "We'll never know." I'm not one of them. I think we may know, but I believe many will reject the truth when they hear it, finding it distasteful.

So the question is: Why are some people not healed despite having received prayer from faith-filled believers, who know their authority and who otherwise have good results?

The most likely explanation for failed healing is a lack of faith in the person praying. I've had many people tell me that they've prayed in faith, but nothing happened. When I ask what kind of results they typically have – they admit that most of the people they pray for are not healed.

If you aren't seeing people healed regularly, the most likely explanation is that you lack the kind of faith that consistently heals people. This kind of faith is covered in the chapter on faith for healing.

The next thing to consider is that some obstacle may be present that must be removed. Sometimes it's a spirit of sickness; sometimes it's fear or an attitude toward God or themselves that must change.

I've heard stories about failed healing from people who asked if they might pray with someone they knew. In these cases, the one needing healing held the one praying in low esteem or had other negative feelings that the one praying was able to sense. In these cases, healing did not manifest.

Our perceptions of the one praying can be an obstacle to receiving healing. Our view of them can create doubt in their mind or build a barrier in our heart that prevents us from receiving our healing. This is particularly true if we hold ill feelings toward them or someone else. Remember that James tied confession of sin and forgiveness to healing.

Mindsets Among Healers

I'm a creature of habit. One of my habits is finding patterns in things. I'm not sure that I do it intentionally, but it seems like I notice patterns more than most people. In my time on Facebook, I've noticed patterns of behavior and beliefs among the thousands of friends I have. People who have these behaviors fall into groups, at least in my mind, and sometimes they form literal groups. There are three groups of people that regularly interact with me.

Two of these groups operate in divine healing. The groups have their origin in two divergent views about how healing is to be done. One group existed long before the other one. Although the first group has a lot of truth in its teaching about healing, it also has some misunderstanding and error. As these errors were recognized, a second group formed which took note of the errors and developed new doctrines about healing that were supposed to be free of them. In an attempt to completely strip the first group of any credibility, the second group tossed out nearly all the teachings of the first group, including the legitimate things they had discovered. We now have two groups that operate in healing which seem to have become adversaries. Now let's look at each group.

The first group tends to approach healing from a revelatory standpoint. They desire to have God reveal the issues involved in a person's life that contribute to their condition and through a process of dealing with each issue, healing takes place. They look at issues of sin and repentance, generational curses, and problems that exist in the soul. They have good results in the areas of inner healing and deliverance and some success in physical healing.

The second group for the most part rejects the need for God to reveal issues in a person's life. They operate instead by exercising faith and authority over sickness. There is little else they rely on to accomplish healing. Because of this view, they tend to attribute failure in healing to a lack of faith or a lack of exercising authority. They rarely consider other possibilities. And although they have impressive results in the area of physical healing, they don't do as well in the area of emotional healing, though they agree that 100 percent healing is the goal.

Both groups have a measure of success and a measure of failure, but neither group sees everyone healed. It's been said, "If your only tool is a hammer, everything looks like a nail." I think both groups suffer from working with a small toolbox. Each group could learn a great deal from the other and probably have better success, but this never seems to happen. Both groups are highly suspicious of the other and frankly, there's a lot of hostility between them. Sadly, the hostility is instigated and encouraged by the leaders in each group.

The third group is small; just a handful of people who receive healing prayer as often as possible from people in both groups but their illness remains. Most of these illnesses manifest as physical symptoms. Often their symptoms confound medical experts and defy diagnostic tests. They're often told, "We can't find anything in our tests," or they receive a diagnosis like fibromyalgia, which puts a name on the condition, but doesn't explain its cause. (There are many theories about what might cause fibromyalgia, but there is no consensus among medical experts at this time.) While other people with serious illness gradually get better or experience a sudden miracle, these individuals often suffer continual disappointment, never getting better and some actually become worse. They always ask, "Why?"

I've seen patterns in this group as well. It seems like many of these people have gone through times of emotional trauma without being completely healed of the painful memories from their past. In addition to the memories, there are a host of feelings they struggle with like helplessness, worthlessness, rejection, fear, bitterness, mistrust and loneliness. Some of them clearly appear to suffer from some demonic oppression. I believe at least one contributing factor to the failure of their physical healing is their failed emotional and spiritual healing.

What they desire most is physical healing from the symptoms of disease. What they seem to want least is to re-live the events of their past and go through the emotions again, or to be involved in what could become a lengthy or dramatic deliverance and inner healing process. Most have found a way to endure their emotional trauma and keep going in spite of their physical sickness. I believe it is God's ultimate desire for all of us to be healed, set free and walking in the truth. God is interested in our complete healing; body, spirit and soul; in a word; *sozo*.

"Sozo" is one of the Greek words found in the New Testament that is translated as "healing". When we use the term sozo, we're talking about something that's more than just physical healing. In fact, sozo contains the idea of physical healing but it is much broader in scope. It means to:

- Save
- Keep safe and sound
- Rescue from danger or destruction
- Rescue from injury or peril
- Save from suffering or disease
- Make well
- Heal
- Restore to health.

If someone is healed of an illness affecting the physical body, we refer to it as physical healing. If they receive deliverance from an evil spirit, it's a spiritual healing. If they're healed of post-traumatic stress disorder, it's an emotional healing. If they were to be healed of all three, we're describing something referred to as being made "whole," which is the idea behind the word "sozo."

Jon Sellers and other friends have taught me the importance of wholeness and the fact that God is just as concerned about our spiritual and mental health as our physical health, even if we are not. Let me rephrase that; God cares more about our emotional healing than we do. The same is true for spiritual healing. The problem is that some of us care too much about the physical healing we want and not enough about the spiritual and emotional healing we need. The fact is that our physical condition may require emotional and spiritual healing to be completed first. Why do I believe this?

There are two reasons. The first is that some physical diseases have demonic (spiritual) origins. As we've seen with the woman who was bent over for 18 years and the boy with seizures who was deaf and mute. Both had physical symptoms that required deliverance from a spirit before they could be healed. Many people who only desire to be physically healed, are actually in need of deliverance (spiritual healing) first. And because this has not occurred, they remain unhealed and tormented by the enemy.

The other reason is just a hunch. God wants everyone to be healed in every way. Strange as it may sound, some people only want to be healed of a disease or condition that causes physical pain. They have no great desire to be healed of painful emotions or memories. They're willing to put up with feelings of fear, rejection and other emotional wounds because they see them as just another part of life. But God wants us to be free of those things as well.

Perhaps God knows that if we were to be healed of our physical sickness, we might never seek healing of the unforgiveness that poisons our soul or the spirit of fear that attacks us at night. The wisdom of God may allow our physical healing to manifest only after the spiritual and emotional problems are dealt with as a way to assure that in the end, we are completely healed. What good is a healed body connected to a bitter, unforgiving heart? What benefit is a sound tummy to someone plagued by a spirit of fear that dominates their every thought?

I think what these people need most is not more prayer over their physical symptoms, but the completion of their emotional and spiritual healing which, if it were to happen, would result in their physical healing being completed. Many of us need some degree of deliverance and others need inner healing to take place before any long-term physical healing will happen.

The pain of dealing with the past may prevent us from facing those problems and resolving them. The healing that God desires for us may require us to do things we'd rather not, like facing bitterness, rejection, unforgiveness, fear, abandonment, shame, etc. Submitting ourselves to God and surrendering our right to allow these things to remain is a process. As long as we allow them to remain, they'll hold us captive and the spirits of infirmity will have a hold on us that can't be broken, no matter how many people pray for us to be healed.

One definition of insanity is doing the same thing over and over and expecting different results. I'm all for persistence in prayer. I'm convinced that some things just take time. But those cases are the ones where gradual progress is being made. If we pray and pray and absolutely no progress is made or the person seems to be getting worse, and there are obvious signs that emotional healing or deliverance are needed, it's foolish to continue on the same course. In such cases we must consider using other tools. This might require us to discover tools we haven't heard of, or perhaps use tools that we had previously rejected or dismissed.

If we are to walk as Jesus walked and do the things He did, we might consider the novel, peculiar and sometimes bizarre methods He used. I don't think Jesus avoided predictable formulas just to confound us. I believe He continually asked His Father for the best solution to the problem, not assuming it would be the same as the previous one. His openness to the leading of the Father was the thing that gave Him such a consistent life of victory. If it worked for Him, it should work for us.

CHAPTER TWENTY-FIVE

Fasting

WHEN I REFER TO FASTING in this chapter, I'm speaking of abstaining from eating certain foods or drinking certain beverages for a period of time for spiritual reasons. Although some people abstain from things like watching television and refer to it as fasting, that is not what I would consider fasting for the purpose of this discussion.

Looking at what the Bible says about fasting, it's apparent that it has been done in different ways in the past. Some people seemed to have fasted only once or twice over a long period of time – typically forty days. Moses, Elijah and Jesus fasted this way (see Ex. 34:28, 1 Kgs. 19:8 and Lk. 4:1-2). Daniel fasted for 21 days before receiving a vision of future events from the angel Michael (see Dan. 10:3). But not everyone mentioned in scripture followed these examples. Some made a habit to fast frequently, for shorter periods of time. The apostle Paul, the disciples of John the Baptist, Cornelius and Anna, the woman who served at the temple all fasted often and for short periods of time (see Mt. 9:14, 2 Cor. 11:27, Acts 10:30 and Lk. 2:37).

Many instances of fasting are recorded in the Old Testament. They generally had to do with the death of a beloved person, times of prayer and intercession for approaching military conflicts and for divine guidance in personal and public affairs. Fewer are recorded in the New Testament, but fasting was done when decisions were made concerning the appointing of elders (see Acts 14:23) and when the disciples were instructed by the Holy Spirit to send Paul and Barnabas on their missionary journey (see Acts 13:2).

Fasting and Healing

When someone asks me if they should fast, I usually say, "It depends." Whether or not a person should fast depends on what they want to accomplish. Since most of the people who ask are merely interested in healing a few people my answer is often, "no." It isn't necessary to fast before you can heal the sick. Jesus gave His disciples authority over all the power of the enemy and this authority encompasses healing. It is not dependent on fasting. Fasting is not *required* before you can see the sick healed.

Because Jesus told the disciples that the demon in the epileptic boy would not come out except through prayer and fasting (see Mt. 17:21), some have taught that it is necessary to spend time praying and fasting before you can heal the sick or cast out demons. While fasting may be helpful to accomplish certain things related to healing, I don't believe it's absolutely necessary. The disciples were able to heal many people in spite of the fact that they apparently had not done much fasting.

For the believer interested in healing, one advantage of fasting is that it helps put to death the flesh. The *flesh* is a biblical term for our bodily desires. Our spirit and our flesh are constantly at war with each other (see Gal. 5:17). When we're hungry, we eat, which feeds our body and keeps our flesh happy and more or less in control of things. When we fast, the goal is to decrease the dominion our bodily desires have over the power of our spirit man. When we fast, our spirit man becomes stronger and more dominant. A stronger spirit is more aware of God's presence and that creates greater faith and confidence in what He wants to accomplish.

Fasting has developed a bad reputation in some circles. Many people who operate successfully in healing are strongly opposed to fasting. Others believe it's essential to spend time fasting before the sick can be healed. Beliefs about fasting have been taken to extremes in both directions. Personally, I think the truth lies somewhere in the middle. The biblical narrative on fasting isn't crystal clear, which may account for the disagreement people have. You could support almost any view on fasting using the right verses of Scripture.

Some teach that fasting was part of the old covenant and as such, it has no application today, because we live under a new covenant. Their objection is that fasting, because it is done as a ritual in order to keep the law, can become a form of legalism. In this assertion, they are correct. If we believe that fasting or any of our acts will impress God, we are mistaken (see Rom. 3:28). Keeping rules and performing rituals will never make us righteous in God's eyes. Fasting that is done to maintain or earn a righteous standing with God is useless. But this isn't the only reason for fasting and God is always interested in the motives behind our actions.

Fasting may be seen not as an attempt to keep the law, but as a spiritual principle used to accomplish certain things. There are principles taught in the Scriptures that are eternal spiritual principles which bear fruit to those who desire their benefits, and I believe fasting is one of them. Moses, Elijah and Jesus all spent long periods of time fasting. They heard God's voice more clearly than anyone of their day and collectively, they worked countless miracles. Jesus performed no miracles until after He spent 40 days fasting in the wilderness (see Mt. 4:2).

The western world seems to be wedded to a lifestyle of eating. How do we deal with the problem of eating meals at work? Some of us eat at the nearest café, some carry containers of food to work and many of us forage on whatever we can find in break rooms. I'm as guilty as anyone. The hospitals put out free chips, sandwiches and cookies in their EMS rooms. Some provide free meals in their cafeterias. Our skylines are littered with fast food restaurants screaming for our attention. For some, eating is no longer a means to provide fuel for the body. It's become an obsession, a ritual, and an expensive lifestyle.

We need an awareness of our lifestyle if we ever hope to make changes to it. The apostle Paul said we shouldn't be conformed to the world's ways, but we should be transformed by the renewing of our minds (see Rom. 12:2). If we are to grow and develop a lifestyle of healing, we must consider our present way of living and admit two things: few of us actually hear God as clearly as we'd like to, and we don't see the kind of victory over the enemy that we hope for.

In the Sermon on the Mount, recorded in Matthew chapter 6, Jesus taught His disciples how to pray. Immediately following this, He taught them how to fast:

> *"When you fast, do not be like the hypocrites, with a sad countenance. For they disfigure their faces that they may appear to men to be fasting. Assuredly, I say to you, they have their reward. But you, when you fast, anoint your head and wash your face, so that you do not appear to men to be fasting, but to your Father who is in the secret place; and your Father who sees in secret will reward you openly."*
> MT. 6:16-18

Jesus taught His disciples how to fast in this passage, but according to the disciples of John the Baptist, they didn't make a habit of fasting (see Mt. 9:14). The disciples were able to heal the sick and cast out demons without fasting, that is, until they failed to heal the boy with seizures. When they asked why they failed, Jesus said it was because of unbelief. He then said their unbelief resulted from their failure to spend time in prayer and fasting (see Mt. 17:21). The implication here is that if the disciples had obeyed His teaching and spent time in prayer and fasting, they may have had the faith needed to cast the demon out.

From this, I would conclude that fasting is neither essential, nor useless. Fasting could be seen as optional for the believer interested in healing. It wasn't required for the disciples to heal the sick and cast out most of the demons they encountered. Likewise, most of the healing and deliverance we'll do can be done without fasting. But there are certain adversaries that require greater faith to conquer. That level of faith may come only through prayer and fasting. If healing a few people once in a while is your goal, it probably isn't necessary to fast. But if you plan to do warfare against demons on a regular basis, it may afford you an advantage.

Jesus didn't create a long list of rules about fasting. He kept it simple; when you fast, don't make a public show of it and don't be a hypocrite. Fasting isn't about looking spiritual or impressing anyone. It's between you and the Father. He left the specifics up to them.

Medical Views of Fasting

There are a wide range of metabolic changes and emotional experiences people have when fasting. The benefits include a heightened spiritual awareness and relaxation of the body, mind, and emotions. During fasting, the blood and lymphatic systems are detoxified. Toxins from the colon, kidneys, bladder, lungs, sinuses, and skin can also be removed by the body.

The decreased consumption of calories during fasting has significant effects on the body. Because of the lack of glucose consumed, the liver converts stored glycogen into glucose which supplies energy for the body. The brain and the central nervous system have a high demand for glucose. When stored glycogen is used up, they must get it either from the breakdown of proteins or fatty acids. The body is resistant to breaking down proteins, so fatty acids are converted into ketones, and they become the primary source of energy. The build up of ketones in the blood can be a problem and it may be averted by drinking fruit juice, which will provide carbohydrates for energy and cellular function.

Short-term, intermittent fasting has become a widely accepted way to rid the body of toxins. Short-term fasts (48 hours or less) can usually be done without medical supervision. For longer fasts, doctors typically recommend a physical examination and they may suggest monitoring of biochemical changes. Thousands of website testimonials cover the success stories of people who have fasted.

Fasting does have hazards you should be aware of. Side effects can include weakness, headaches, nausea, and muscle aches. Everyone responds to fasting differently. While one individual may become sick immediately after beginning a fast, another person may feel energized and renewed. There are rare side effects that can occur during long term fasting. These side effects include a drop in blood pressure, a persistent cold, and emotional distress. If these symptoms persist, the fast should be stopped. A prolonged fast can lead to anemia, impairment of liver function, kidney stones, mineral imbalances, ketosis and other undesirable side effects. Deaths due to prolonged fasting have occurred, though they are not common.

My Experiences

I have had about as many failures as I've had victories in the area of fasting. But with every fall, I learned something about myself and about God, and I haven't regretted any of it. Fasting is a very personal thing. Your experiences will be different from mine. My assignments, my gifts and my calling are different from yours. What you get out of fasting will depend on what God has called you to do.

I first tried fasting years ago during a difficult time of my life. I felt like I needed to hear God's voice during a time of testing and trials. My first fast was for one day. It didn't seem that difficult. Since then, I've talked with friends who felt like they were going to die trying to go one day without eating. Everyone is different. I may have had an advantage. I had been working 24-hour shifts as a paramedic for about 20 years. I've often been so busy responding to calls that I didn't have time to eat. My mind may have received prior training that helped me with the discipline of fasting.

My second fast was for three days. That was more difficult, but I made it, drinking only water. The hardest part was ignoring my stomach, which grumbled continually. At the end of the third day, I did feel slightly less earth-bound, and I began to sense God's voice a little more clearly. A week or so after this I fasted for six days, eating no food, drinking only water and some juice. As I progressed further into the time of fasting, God's voice became easier to discern and the tug and pull of the cares of the world grew faint. After three days, the sensation of hunger left. Resisting the urge to eat on days four, five and six was easy. I spent time alone on day six, asking things of God and listening for answers. When I was satisfied that I had all the information I needed, I began eating again. Most people notice their hunger sensations dissipate during the first three days of fasting.

I didn't fast again for a couple of years. I didn't feel a need for it, but God did. He tried in different ways to alert me to the need for fasting, but I was unaware of it. He finally got my attention and I began once again, gradually working my way up to longer periods of fasting. That's one of the points I'd like to suggest. Begin with a reachable goal and after you succeed – go a little longer the next time. I found that doubling the length of time was a reasonable goal for me. I began at one day, then three, then six, then 12. The longest I've fasted so far is 19 days.

I prefer to fast without eating any type of solid food and generally just drink water. That's just my personal preference. I have a friend who did a 21-day "Daniel Fast" which is similar to a vegetarian diet. (Information about this fast is readily available online and in books.) He had great results and began having visions and powerful dreams during and after the time of fasting. My wife prefers to make a vegetable broth when she fasts. Some people skip one meal a day on a certain day of the week and others fast the entire day. If you work long hours, you might want to fast at work and eat at home. If you feel weak or dizzy while fasting, check your blood sugar. If you have diabetes, liver problems or other health issues, consult your doctor before fasting.

I'd like to suggest a few things about listening to God. Be very aware of what He is saying during this time, and be obedient to whatever He asks of you. Drawing closer to God should always be the focus of fasting. Several times while I was fasting, God gave me instructions and I tried to dismiss it as the enemy talking to me.

After feeling like I should take a few mineral supplements to prevent leg cramps, God told me to stop taking them. I didn't listen. So He gave me a dream about buying mango, pineapple and orange juice at a store. In the dream, the worship leader, Paul Baloche was working behind the counter. This told me the dream was from God. I stopped taking the supplements and bought juice the next day and never had leg cramps. God has told me to stop fasting before the time I chose to stop. Naturally, I rebuked the evil spirit, and continued on my holy quest. Eventually, God spoke loudly enough to convince me that I was just being disobedient.

Matt Sorger has given some good advice on fasting: "Don't forget to pray – otherwise it's just a diet." I was guilty of ignoring God completely while fasting for 5 days. I was busy doing other things. During that fast I never spent more than a few minutes at a time thinking about God or seeking His instruction. It was a waste of time, except that I learned to pursue God more diligently the next time. God can tell you when it's time to fast, so ask Him. He gave me a dream about fasting, which I'll share:

In the dream, I was preparing for a trip. I created a special pillow made of memory foam. I added another pillow inside the pillowcase. I was telling some friends about it. I also had a water bottle with a removable panel that had two parts to it. Another guy had the same bottle. In the dream, we were washing the bottles. I was explaining to him how to clean the bottle thoroughly. Finally, I was in front of a mirror and I noticed I had really flat abs – no spare tire at all, and I was very tan.

There were four things in this dream that spoke about fasting:

1. The water bottle speaks of fasting, because I carry one with me when I fast.

2. The "memory foam" pillow speaks of fasting because God increases revelation through dreams when I fast. "Memory foam" refers to committing my dreams to memory by journaling them.

3. Flat abs speaks of fasting because I lose one to two pounds a day while fasting and my abdominal muscles become more prominent.

4. Going on a trip symbolizes the spiritual journey we take while fasting.

Weight loss is inevitable when you fast. How much you'll lose depends on your metabolism, activity and method of fasting. I'll warn you – the weight you lose during fasting is even easier to put back on afterward, unless you make it a routine or alter your lifestyle following the time of fasting.

If you're single, fasting can be done independently as often as you choose, with little regard for the needs of others. If you're part of a family that has a routine of eating meals together, having one person who doesn't eat *can* be a problem. Discuss your plans for fasting with your family and come to an understanding before starting. Having your spouse join you in fasting may be a good option.

I'll close with this final story. The time that I fasted for 19 days was an incredible experience. After 12 days, I began to hear God's voice very clearly. After 18 days I heard Him constantly. All day long, wherever I went, God was speaking to me as clearly as anyone else. I didn't hear an audible voice, but it was a clearly discernible inner voice. I had the most amazing dreams and I began to have visions every time I closed my eyes. He gave me a private Bible study from a couple of different chapters. The first was from Genesis. He spoke about how before the fall, He and Adam had a relationship like I was experiencing during the time I fasted. He told me that this was how our relationship was intended to be from the beginning. He went on to explain that it was my choice to enter into this experience, and I could go as deep in it as I wanted to. There were many other things He told me that morning.

I am not a physician. This chapter is not intended to be used in place of medical advice from a doctor. I would encourage you to research fasting on your own to see if it's for you. Please consult your doctor before you consider fasting.

CHAPTER TWENTY-SIX

Recording the Testimony

SOME OF US STRUGGLE WITH sharing testimonies about healing. While most of us want to share our stories about the work of God that we witness, many of us fear being filled with pride or we fear being put on a pedestal by others. I've wrestled with these problems, too. When God suggested that I would work miracles through His power, I was both excited and a little fearful. The thrill of seeing the awesome power of God at work is no small thing. But I've lived with constant fear of being taken captive by pride or being exalted by people as some kind of spiritual guru they should follow after.

Four years ago while arguing with myself about whether or not to start a blog about healing, I woke up several mornings in a row at 4:20. I thought perhaps God was trying to send me a message, but I didn't know what it was. The third time it happened I decided to ask Him if He was waking me up at this exact time every day for a purpose.

I sensed His suggestion to look for the answer in the book of Acts. In chapter four, verse twenty, (4:20) I found this:

"For we cannot but speak the things which we have seen and heard."

I took this as confirmation that I should move forward. I began a blog about healing, despite the fact that I'd never seen anyone healed yet. Authoring the blog helped me learn about healing and share information with others. In watching other people operate in healing and hearing their testimonies, I began to believe I might be able to do it, too. One of my goals was to share with as many people as possible what God was doing. But I wasn't reaching many people. What's the point of writing if you have no readers? I considered using social networking and decided to create a Facebook profile. Within a few months, the blog had ten times more readers, but it created a more visible, public profile and that's been a source of concern for me.

In getting the testimonies out I've been plagued with worries about pride. I sometimes wonder if my attempts to gain readers might really be a veiled attempt to gain popularity and acceptance. There is an ever-present question lurking in the back of my mind: "Am I really bringing glory to God, or am I doing this for myself?"

Testimonies are a part of training and equipping the Church. Those who don't yet have faith for healing can be encouraged by watching successful healers at work and by hearing their testimonies. I found someone whose testimonies greatly encouraged me and I devoured everything I could find that showed him in operation. The more I studied his teaching, the more I developed boldness in approaching strangers on the street. His name is Todd White and his testimonies have been a great inspiration for me. Hearing the testimonies of others also gives hope to those who need healing. If we never share the miracles of God, why would anyone expect to be healed?

There are many ways in which people share their testimonies. Some use video, some do it by status updates on Facebook, some have blogs, some write books, and others share their stories in person. There doesn't seem to be one way that is best. They're all effective. In sharing healing testimonies some healers display true humility and meekness, while others seem to be filled with pride. I recently read a confession from a man who had a successful healing ministry. He publicly admitted to exaggerating and falsifying healing testimonies. Although he'd seen many legitimate miracles, he disqualified his valid testimonies with false ones. Some people excel in giving glory to God while others appear to be building their own fan clubs. And some people do a marvelous job of presenting the simple truth of God's power and love without a lot of baggage.

I have a few problems sharing testimonies of the things I've witnessed. The battle I have with pride is one problem and privacy is another. I work in medicine and I pray for my patients. Health care laws restrict what can be shared without the consent of my patients. If I were to post a video or photo of a patient, I could get in trouble. My freedom to share testimonies is somewhat restricted, but God still wants me to testify. He gave me a dream to illustrate this point.

In the dream I was going from place to place recording the testimonies of the different things God had done. I took statements from people who were healed or who witnessed some other work of God. In some cases I had seen them healed and in others I didn't. Most of the testimonies involved healing, but not all. I felt a very strong sense of purpose in the dream. This wasn't something I did for myself, it was important to God and I knew these testimonies would last into eternity.

What struck me as strange was the fact that some of the stories I recorded were a second testimony to replace ones that had been destroyed. I knew in the dream that every testimony was very important and none of them were to be discarded or ignored. This was the basic content of the dream.

One thing God revealed in the dream is the fact that the enemy is not only trying to prevent the work of God, but he is trying to destroy and discredit our testimonies. The other thing is that our testimonies are extremely important to Him.

If you study the patriarchs of Israel, you'll note that whenever God did something amazing for them, or when He revealed something of Himself they'd never seen before, an enduring landmark was built. Often a pile of stones was erected which served as a reminder to future generations of the works that God had done.

The Lord asked Moses to build a portable box called an ark in which the nation of Israel would carry three things – the tablets of the law given to Moses on Mount Sinai, a jar full of the manna that God provided as their food when they lived in the wilderness for 40 years, and the staff of Aaron, which miraculously sprouted buds. The contents of the ark were an ever-present reminder to them about who their God was and what He had done. Our testimony today serves the exact same purpose.

Testimonies of what God has done through us are between Him and us. The issue of pride is between Satan and us. We shouldn't let the issue of pride stand in the way of our responsibility. God requires us to testify. It's up to us to do it with humility and integrity. No doubt everyone used by God will struggle with pride from time to time. We need to confidently walk in our identity as sons and daughters in the kingdom. But we also need to walk in the humble knowledge that it is the Lord and not us, who is on display. We are merely instruments in His hands.

CHAPTER TWENTY-SEVEN

The Future of Healing

THE TREND TOWARD EVERYDAY PEOPLE operating in divine healing isn't slowing down – it's gaining momentum. What started out as an oddity has become a powerful movement. God has given me a number of dreams foretelling what the future of healing might look like.

On June 8th in 2010 I had a dream that contained two scenes. In the first scene I watched a presentation in which a new kind of airplane module was being demonstrated. It was built using advanced technology. The module was designed to withstand any type of crash. It held a small crew of no more than five people. The crew that would occupy this module received diverse training, but their primary function was as a medical team. They were given advanced equipment to use for their mission. The module was to be retrofitted to all passenger airliners. In the dream, it was a known fact that airliners would be crashing in the future. The retrofit of the module was to ensure the survival of a handful of people when the airplanes crashed. Once an airplane crashed, the module would separate from the airplane fuselage and open. The crew would be unharmed by the impact. They would get out of the module and survive wherever they were.

Part of the demonstration I watched in the dream explained the training the crew went through, which allowed them to survive, even in the most hostile environment. It was known to everyone that the airplanes would crash in hostile territory. This was the end of the first part of the dream. In the second part, I watched the technology for the new module being developed. It was a very long and detailed dream. I didn't recall any of those details.

Interpretation

In dreams, commercial airliners typically represent large groups of people, either within the church or in society. A crash represents a sudden change that results in the loss of something. The fact that all airliners were going to crash speaks of an event that will impact nearly everyone. The module represents a protective enclosure crafted by God that allows a few individuals to live in close proximity with others, but provides on a moment's notice, isolation from them, and protection from harm. (Perhaps they would need protection from others due to something like increased religious persecution or civil unrest.)

The dream reveals that sudden, major changes are coming to society, the church or both. The cause isn't clear. It seems to be something that will happen suddenly and with little warning. It's important to note that the airplanes crashed at different times, not all at once. I'd interpret this as a series of small events, rather than a single, large one. If the crash speaks of society in general, it may be due to natural disasters or man-made events like war. If the church is the subject, it could portray large scale changes in how the body of Christ meets or functions. The important point is that God is making preparations in anticipation of these events.

The training for the survivors included a variety of disciplines, but the main focus was medicine. Since the dream was symbolic, this is probably not a literal reference to medicine, but a symbolic reference to divine healing.

I've believed for some time that the realm of divine healing, which is optional for most of us today, will become an essential survival tool in the future. It may be that the health care system will ultimately fail, leaving millions of sick people without any treatment, except primitive or natural medicine and divine healing. It may suggest a global war or some large-scale natural disaster. In any case, those who will survive must develop a diversity of tools to work with. The survival teams in my dream went through intense, long hours of training. Perhaps this speaks of operating in all the manifestations of the Spirit like healing, miracles, prophecy, words of knowledge, etc.

A major emphasis in the dream was on "new technology." I believe God has many new things waiting for us. By "new technology" I'm not referring to things that aren't found in the Bible or things that weren't practiced by the early church. In the area of divine healing for example, most of us have only scratched the surface in understanding how to heal people effectively. We have far more questions than answers. I believe God wants to give us the answers we're looking for.

The airplanes crashed in hostile territory. The territory didn't suddenly become hostile. It was always that way. But traveling in the airplanes provided protection and isolation from it. That protection is going to be removed. How that will happen is debatable. The resulting situation will be catastrophic for most of us and difficult, even for those who are prepared for it.

On July 4th in 2010 I had another dream that took place in the distant future. In the dream, divine healing was seen as a scientific and highly organized field. I was a specialist in one type of healing that involved seeing the medical condition of a patient and praying for healing out of what I saw. I had a job in this profession as a healer. When I came to work I would login to a workstation and review a video file of the person's condition that I was going to pray for. I would pray for them from the visions I saw and my prayer was recorded. It became part of their permanent record. Four different specialists were involved in the healing process. Each specialist prayed in a different way. Every patient received prayer from all four kinds of specialists and everyone was healed, without exception.

The number four seemed significant in this dream. The dream occurred on July 4th and each person received prayer from four different specialists. I looked up the number four in *The Prophet's Dictionary* by Paula Price. Here's part of the entry for the number four:

"The number of world impact by way of the four corners of the earth. Prophetically, the number represents something with worldwide impact primarily signifying the four compass points – north, south, east, and west – in its intent or affect."

This dream could be a glimpse at the global state of healing 25 years from now. Unfortunately, many Christians can't imagine Jesus delaying His return that long. We've stood too long looking at the sky, waiting for His return and in doing so, we've lost our vision for the future. Some of us can only see increasing darkness and depravity covering the earth – thinking the return of Jesus is our only hope. I once thought this way. But I don't any longer.

God has given me a vision for the future of healing that is far better than what we see today. It's so grand that it will take more than my lifetime to accomplish everything He wants to do. I've decided to build a legacy in healing that my children and grandchildren can carry on long after I'm gone.

The future of healing has virtually unlimited potential. The only restrictions that exist are those we've created in our minds. Whatever we can imagine as the future of healing, God can accomplish through us because there are no limitations on what He can do. I would encourage you to dream big when it comes to healing. Our past doesn't dictate our future and our future could be far better than we've ever dreamed.

CHAPTER TWENTY-EIGHT

Greater Works

JESUS TOLD HIS DISCIPLES THAT the works they would do would be greater than the works He did:

> *"Most assuredly, I say to you, he who believes in Me, the works that I do he will do also; and greater works than these he will do, because I go to My Father."*
>
> JN. 14:12

During the two millenia that have passed since Jesus spoke these words, they have challenged just about everyone who has read them. Jesus clearly indicated that His disciples would do even greater works than He did. Some people take this not only as a command, but as a prophecy that must be fulfilled. I don't know anyone who has been able to imagine what these "greater works" might look like. What human could ever claim to have done even greater works than Jesus?

Not wanting to deny Scripture, but neither wanting to believe what He said to be true in a literal sense, some people have twisted His words, suggesting an interpretation that explains away the obvious meaning. They explain: "He didn't mean greater works in quality, He meant greater in quantity and since the Church has added countless millions of believers over the millennia, we have fulfilled His calling to do greater works."

What rubbish.

One glance at the Greek text reveals that Jesus was referring to greater works both in quantity *and* quality. The body of Christ has not yet done these greater works. But I believe we will do them before the Lord returns.

A few months before this book manuscript was finished, I received a call from my friend, Michael King. He asked how the writing was going. I told him it was moving along nicely. We talked about a chapter that I'd recently added to the manuscript. He shared a prophetic word, asking that I would be open to one last bit of revelation from God as the completion of the book drew near. He didn't give me any more details – just a cryptic suggestion to be open-minded. Not wanting to miss something important, I asked God to share with me anything else He wanted to include in the book. A few weeks later I had the following dream:

I was standing in a room with other people that I didn't know. We had volunteered for some kind of mission. We had no idea what it involved. A man began to speak with the group. He said he would tell us why we were there, what our mission was and how it would be carried out. He talked at great length about many things, but nothing he said clearly described what the mission was or how it was to be carried out. He gave hints and suggestions here and there in vague terms about what we might do, but he never described anything in detail.

I was confused and bewildered listening to this man who was one of our leaders. After we listened for a while, other men appeared in the room. Their job was to assist in our training. Soon after they entered the room, they began to attack us. Some people were shot and others were beaten. Some tried to hide from the attackers. None of us had weapons and I saw no way out of the building, so I decided to pretend as if I were dead. Two men found me and believing I was dead, they left me and looked for someone else to attack. At this point in the dream, I just wanted to get out of the building. This ended the first scene.

In the second part of the dream, I found myself on a mountaintop in Sweden, with three men I'd never met. The four of us got in a small car and began driving down the steep, snow-covered slopes of the mountain. I was in the rear seat of the car. As the terrain became almost vertical, we traveled at a frightening speed, almost out of control. With the scenery whizzing by, I remember thinking the car was going to flip over and crash. But the car continued on its path, which became a level plateau. We drove for a while saying nothing. But soon, we reached another steep down-hill slope and began to lose control, flying down the mountain at break-neck speed. Again, I remember thinking we were going to flip over and crash, but we didn't. We continued driving the tiny car through the deep snow, hanging on for our lives with no idea where we were going. This was the end of the second scene.

The third and final scene brought the four of us to a countryside dotted with small villages. We weren't in the car any longer. And we weren't walking. Something had happened to us. We had the ability to travel wherever we wanted, merely by willing ourselves to go there. As soon as we decided to go here or there, we quickly went in that direction as if we had no physical body. We were very much like angels. The bodies we inhabited had a luminescence and transparency to them that was similar to the bodies people have reported seeing in heaven.

We traveled quickly to the nearby cities and encountered many people in need. Some needed healing, some deliverance, some were poor and others were hungry. As we encountered each person, we released the resources of heaven that met their need. I would gesture toward a person with my hand and a brilliant flash of multi-colored light exploded above them. As soon as this happened, their need was met and I would find another person in need and do the same for them. The four of us scoured the cities in what seemed like a few minutes, finding everyone in need and taking care of them by releasing the resources of heaven. A brilliant light flashed each time one of us released something from heaven. Nothing was delayed. People and their circumstances were changed in the blink of an eye.

We moved like the wind – without caution and without resistance. We never asked permission to do these marvelous works. As we met one person then another, we immediately knew what had to be done. There was no thought involved. We never questioned whether God wanted to bless them or if it was right to heal them or cast out an evil spirit. We instinctively knew that everything we did was in perfect harmony with the will of the Father and was well-pleasing to Him.

We encountered no enemies that I was aware of. If there were any, they must have been invisible or hidden. The light and the glory of God that accompanied us made it impossible to see the presence of darkness or evil. All we could see was the constant release of the light and power of God as it flashed before our eyes everywhere we went. This was how the dream ended.

I'd like to interpret the dream and make the application of it at the same time.

"I had volunteered for an assignment..."

All believers come to Christ voluntarily. Some come seeking forgiveness, others because Jesus and His death provide some meaning to the riddle of life. Some are set free of addiction. Still others come to Jesus in their last breath before dying. None of them know at the outset what they've signed up for. The opening scene is a portrait of believers coming into the kingdom of God, but their entrance is first into the building that is often called "the church." The building where people gather on Sunday is not "the church." The church is the living, breathing, collection of people in whom the Spirit of God lives.

"A man began to speak with the group..."

The leader who promised to explain why we were there but never did was symbolic of Church leaders who talk about spiritual things but don't understand how the kingdom of God operates. Most seminaries do not train leaders to heal the sick, cast out demons or raise the dead.

Leaders who are not properly trained themselves, have little to offer others. In the end, their talk only creates more confusion.

"Soon after they entered the room, they began to attack us…"

The attacks that the new volunteers suffered portray (symbolically) the harsh treatment some Christians receive from their brothers. Some churches have allowed gossip, slander and every form of hatred to be perpetrated by one believer against another. Sadly, some leaders who are called to nurture and protect believers are guilty of some of the worst attacks. In the dream, I desperately wanted to get out of the building, knowing it had become unsafe. Because of the wounds we inflict on one another, some believers leave the church shortly after receiving Christ as their savior. In the dream, God granted my request and removed me from the building, taking me to a safer place.

"I found myself on a mountaintop…"

The prophet Daniel interpreted the dream of king Nebuchadnezzar, telling him that four kingdoms would rule over the earth and that one day a great kingdom would be established by the God of heaven that would destroy all other kingdoms. This kingdom was symbolized by a mountain (see Dan. 2:35,44). God often uses the imagery of mountains to speak about things of the kingdom.

At the time of this writing, I live outside of Phoenix, Arizona – a desert paradise surrounded by sand and cacti. It would be hard to imagine a place more unlike my home than a mountaintop in Sweden. The symbolism here suggests that if God removes you from the building known as "the church," He may take you to a place and a lifestyle far removed from your comfort zone and He may connect you with people whose language you don't understand. These things may be literal, but they are certainly symbolic of the odd way in which kingdom-minded people operate when compared to the rest of the world.

"The four of us got in a small car…"

In dreams, vehicles often illustrate some aspect of the ministry we're involved in. The small car may suggest one with small beginnings.

Once again the number four appears. The four men who rode in the car could symbolize the same concept the number four did in the last chapter – an event with a global impact. Snow is white and clean symbolizing the simplicity, purity and the light of our heavenly calling.

"..and began driving down the steep, snow-covered slopes of the mountain."

The downhill drive illustrates the effortless way in which the kingdom of God operates. It isn't necessary to try to make a car go downhill. Gravity does the work. In a similar way, the kind of life Jesus lived doesn't come through effort. Instead, it comes when we allow the power of the Holy Spirit to flow through us. The small car portrays the kind of life a person in pursuit of the kingdom might live. It isn't flashy or grand, but rather ordinary on the surface. As God trains us in the lifestyle of the supernatural, it might seem like things are moving too quickly and at times like they are out of control, but we must trust that God knows what He is doing and where we are going. The journey toward the fullness of the heavenly calling is a wild adventure.

The final scene portrays the kinds of things God would have us doing. I would humbly suggest that this scene illustrates the "greater works" Christ spoke of. Jesus was the greatest mystic of all time, but His walking on water, passing through walls and the countless miracles He did were just a glimpse of what is possible for us. He said, "All things are possible to him who believes" (see Mk. 9:23).

"We traveled quickly to the nearby cities and encountered many people in need..."

The call of every disciple of Jesus is to *go* into the world and release the power and provision of the kingdom of God.

"I would gesture toward a person... and a brilliant flash of multi-colored light exploded above them."

I believe this scene reveals what is taking place in the invisible realm of the spirit when we pray for people. Few of us are able to see God's supernatural work of healing as it happens. And because we can't see it – we often assume nothing is happening when we pray for someone who shows no outward signs of healing. But if we were able to see in the spirit, we would be amazed.

When we pray even the smallest, most feeble prayer for someone – we release a measure of God's glory upon the one we're praying for. The release of His glory was seen in the flashes of light. When we pray for someone angels are released to combat evil spirits that are harassing them, wounds inflicted by the enemy are visibly healed in their spirit and the countenance of their spirit is visibly changed, even if nothing appears to be happening outwardly. I've seen these things happen when I pray for people. Blake Healy's book *The Veil* confirmed the things I've seen and it gave me a better understanding of what actually takes place in the spiritual realm when I pray.

"The bodies we inhabited had a luminescence and transparency to them..."

When our spiritual bodies are viewed from the spirtual realm, they are very different in appearance from the ones we see in the mirror. Our spiritual bodies are not made up of matter, but of light. They are not made of the photons of light that are visible to the naked eye – but the the spiritual light of eternity that cannot be seen except by our spirits.

The last scene of the dream reveals how we move and interact with things in the spiritual realm. Contrary to the clumsy, awkward way in which we sometimes move in our physical bodies, our spirits move effortlesssly most of the time. Our spiritual bodies are able to release the power and provision of heaven without even thinking about them.

Most people's spiritual bodies have weapons attached to them that the individuals are not aware of. Many of us carry spiritual swords as part of our armament. These weapons are used against evil spirits when they try to attack us. If you were able to see your spiritual body as it really looks from the spiritual perspective you see a strikingly beautiful, yet formidable heavenly being.

"Nothing was delayed. People and their circumstances were changed in the blink of an eye."

A day is coming when everyone we touch will be healed, delivered and made whole. In that day, we won't ask for words of knowledge, we'll know that the sick must be healed. We won't ask God to multiply bread; we'll hand out bread to feed all who are hungry, never doubting that there will be some left over. We will take no money as we travel. We will know that God has provided in advance for all of our expenses. We will travel the ancient highways of the kingdom, being taken in the spirit from town to town without walking or driving. The Lord himself will move us like the wind. In all these things, we will fulfill the prophecy Jesus gave and we will indeed do greater works than He.

I pray that your spiritual eyes would be opened to the assignments to which God has called you. I pray that your heart would be filled with the purest love for God, and that your mind would be renewed to the truth of His kingdom. I pray that you would know the surpassing riches and treasure He has held in reserve for us from the beginning. I pray that you would be filled with all faith, confident in all things, knowing the will of God and demonstrating His power. And I pray that in all these things God would be glorified.